THE LANCASHIRE & YORKSHIRE RAILWAY

RAILWAY

THEN & NOW

THE
LANCASHIRE & YORKSHIRE RAILWAY

THEN & NOW

ALAN EARNSHAW

Ian Allan Publishing

Contents

First published 1992

ISBN 0 7110 2058 2

Published by Ian Allan Ltd, Shepperton, Surrey; and printed by Ian Allan Printing Ltd at their works at Coombelands in Runnymede, England.

Previous page:
A 'Black 5' 4-6-0 No 45371 heads a nine-coach extra through Ashton-under-Lyne.
Kenneth Field

Preface

Exactly 150 years ago, a magnificently engineered railway opened across the Pennine hills of northern England. Not only was it one of the first railways ever to tackle such formidable terrain, but it also had one very unique claim to fame - for it linked together the counties of Lancashire and Yorkshire. Though there had been roads and (later) canals, passing between the two counties for many years, this was the first real means of commodious transport. Interestingly, it also began a gradual break-down of the animosity which had existed between Yorkshiremen and Lancastrians for centuries. In many ways, this railway was one of the major instruments in truly linking the white rose to the red.

However, when it was first conceived social implications were un-thought of, and to its promoters it was purely seen as the means of a rapid form of transport between Manchester and Leeds. Additionally, when the railway began its 'trans-Pennine' service on 1 March 1841, few people would have imagined the extent to which it would expand. Gradually the company spread its 'metals' across the two counties, and after amalgamating with several minor railways, in July 1847 the name of Lancashire & Yorkshire Railway was authorised by Parliament.

Almost three-quarters of a century later the L&YR's automomy ended when it was merged into the LNWR on 31 December 1921, but by then it had grown into one of the largest 'local' railways in the country. Not only did it connect the eastern and western coasts of northern England, its tentacles also spread across the North and Irish seas by means of a large shipping fleet offering regular sailings from ports like Fleetwood, Goole, Liverpool, Preston and Hull.

Though much of the old L&YR system has vanished in the 70 years which have elapsed, a large proportion of the railway's route-mileage still remains. In fact, despite the widespread change in passenger travel and freight traffic trends, the L&YR has fared much better than many of its contemporaries. When I first expressed an interest in writing this comparative study, a fellow railway historian dismissed the idea as 'a most depressing topic on which to write'. During the 150th year of the first trans-Pennine line I travelled by rail throughout Lancashire and Yorkshire, and in reality found it to be anything but depressing. Though much of the railway's flesh has been stripped away, a substantial skeleton still remains on both sides of the Pennines. Yes, there is much to be negative about; for example, many of the once-proud stations are now reduced to the status of unstaffed halts and bear testimony to the years of neglect. Couple this with the accumulated grime generated by the northern mill towns, then superimpose upon it the mindless vandalism and graffiti so prevalent today and the picture may indeed look un-appetising. However, once the train passes out into the open countryside, whether it be along the coastal plains or in the rugged Pennine valleys, the view is much the same as that enjoyed by our forefathers. I have greatly enjoyed my recent travels around what is left of the Lancashire & Yorkshire Railway, and I hope you enjoy my personal impression of it as it stands today.

Alan Earnshaw
Shepley, West Yorkshire
September 1991

Acknowledgements

In 1950, almost 30 years after the merger of the L&YR with the LNWR, the Lancashire & Yorkshire Railway Society was formed to study, collect and disseminate historical information on the railway. Their fine work continues down to today in the form of regular meetings, newsletters, the *Platform* magazine, and a series of branch line booklets. In more recent years, a Lancashire & Yorkshire Railway Association has been formed to provide another journal discussing the 'Business Line'. Though a relative newcomer, the magazine *Flyer* has already established an excellent reputation for the quality of material and topics it has covered.

Much of the source information for this book has been gathered by fellow members of these societies, and I am very grateful to all those who have assisted in this regard. Their help in preparing this manuscript has been invaluable, as have the hours of patient painstaking research which have gone into individual areas of study, whether it be on topographical or mechanical subjects.

I would particularly like to express my thanks to John Alcock, Phillip Atkins, John Bateman, Michael and Robert Berry, Michael Blakemore, Oliver Carter, Jim Davenport, John Edgington, Martin and Michael Eltham, John Hart, Dave Ibbotson, Ken Longbottom, A. J. Ludlam OBE, Paul Shannon, Tim Shuttleworth, Brian Taylor, Graham Vevers and Graham Yeadon for his assistance with the maps. Also to the many members of the staff and volunteers at the East Lancashire Railway, the Kirklees Light Railway, Steamport, and the West Yorkshire Transport Museum.

In the public and private sectors, I record the assistance provided by both Eastern and London Midland regions of British Rail, along with invaluable up-to-date information from The County Surveyor at Lancashire County Council, and railway officers in the passenger transport authorities of Greater Manchester, Merseyside, and West Yorkshire. A debt of thanks is owed to the record offices, museums, archives and library services of the area - regretfully these are too numerous to mention, but particular thanks go to Rochdale Central Library. Help has been willingly provided by the Bombardier Pro-Rail Ltd, The GMA Group, Mowlem Construction, the Port of Goole Authority and Powell-Duffryn (Standard Wagon) Ltd.

I would also like to pay a very special tribute to Barry Lane and his wife Ann, who have so kindly dealt with my 'numerous' telephone calls whilst checking facts or seeking out certain obscure aspects of the L&YR's history. Finally, it is fitting to acknowledge my deep appreciation to my wife Larraine, and our children Sarah, Bryony, Louise and Peter, for the interest, support and 'knowing' understanding which they have shown over the years.

DEDICATION

With the publisher's permission, I should like to dedicate this book to a young railway enthusiast:

ANDREW WARD

in recognition of his courage and determination.

Introduction

My personal introduction to the Lancashire & Yorkshire Railway was a somewhat painful one, experienced alongside the Meltham branch back in 1957. In those days it was just an ordinary railway line to me, and to my mother it was the best place in the district to pick brambles. However, whilst reaching out for a particularly succulent blackberry I tripped over something and fell head-long into the bushes and set into motion a train of events which was to dictate my future interests in life; for in the midst of the bush I discovered an old 'trespass' sign with the words Lancashire & Yorkshire Railway cast across the top. Regretfully, my first railway relic was to be left where it lay, because my mother quickly hurried me home for antiseptic and sticking plaster.

Though deprived of my souvenir, I began to wonder exactly what this Lancashire & Yorkshire Railway was, for all the trains which came down *my* branch line had British Railways painted on them. I asked at the local station, but the porter didn't know and the goods agent couldn't be bothered with me, yet the clock in his office had the letters L&YR emblazoned across its face. The local library was no better, nor was my history teacher, but this was hardly surprising since a full three and half decades had passed since the L&YR ceased to exist as an independent company. The enigma remained in my mind until the following spring, when a school trip to the old railway museum in York provided the answer and consequently sparked off an interest which has now lasted almost 35 years.

It has often been said that any historical document of real value can only be written by those who have experienced a subject first hand, for only from experience can people compile a contemporary record of the things they have seen. From this standpoint, Eric Mason's *The Lancashire & Yorkshire Railway in the 20th Century* (Ian Allan 1954) has to be one of the most valuable reference works on this railway. Because of publications such as this, a strong interest has grown in the pre-Grouping railways - unfortunately there are very few people left to write such a work today. This present publication was greatly influenced by Mason's work, but it is dedicated to taking a retrospective look at the L&YR, portraying the vivid contrasts between 1921 and 1991. Though I do not have the first-hand knowledge of Mason, I have had the advantage of hindsight having extensively travelled around the remnants of the L&YR in recent months.

The origins of the Lancashire & Yorkshire Railway Company go back to the earliest days of public railways, 1825, the year in which the Stockton & Darlington Railway opened and the Manchester & Leeds and Liverpool & Manchester railways were formed. The publicity surrounding the opening of the L&M, particularly the Rainhill Trials, have often eclipsed the more significant development which took place to the east of

Below left:
The pictures accompanying the introductory chapter are intended to show the changing flavour of motive power on the L&YR system, along with the subsequent changes which followed the Grouping in 1923, Nationalisation in 1948 and after the end of steam in 1968. One of the earliest views which came to hand in our photograph selection was this picture of *Holme*, a member of a class of eighteen 2-4-0 locomotives built in the period 1861-65. The first nine engines were named after directors of the L&YR, but the meaning behind the name *Holme* on this engine is somewhat obscure.
B. C. Lane Collection

Manchester - the railway over the Pennines into Yorkshire.

Communication between the two counties has always been dominated by the high moorlands and their most dominant feature — the weather. The vagaries of a Pennine winter have long been a problem facing travellers, and even today the trans-Pennine railways and roads can come to a sudden grinding halt, including the M62 - the motorway they said would never close. The traditional transport routes between the old West Riding and Manchester avoided the open moors and followed a twisting, winding course through two deep valleys cut at the end of the last ice-age. Therefore, the railway was projected to follow the same route. North of Manchester the line of the M&L would pass through Rochdale and Littleborough up to Summit.

Thereafter it was to descend down Walsden Water to Todmorden whereupon it would turn east and run down the gradually widening Calder Valley. The course of the railway would follow the river almost side by side, until Wakefield where the proposed route curved away northeast to Normanton to make a connection with the North Midland Railway.

Unfortunately, though not unnaturally, this choice of route led the M&L into direct conflict with the Rochdale Canal Company. For the next five years the two rivals were to fight the issue through Parliament, and the Act authorising the line's construction was not to get Royal Assent until 4 July 1836. By the time construction work began, other competitors had cast covetous eyes at the trans-Pennine traffic, and routes were already actively

Left:
The most handsome engines
ever built at Horwich
appeared during George
Hughes' period of office as
CME. The first of his
original, four-cylinder 4-6-0s
(No 1506) rolled out of the
works in June 1908, and by
the following March it had
been followed by a further 19
engines. The class were all
rebuilt in the early 1920s,
and No 1518 is seen at York
shortly after the Grouping.
The train is a Liverpool
express largely made up of
LNWR and early LMS stock,
but includes the 12-wheel
kitchen diner, and has as its
first vehicle an L&YR
'Football' saloon for a private
booking.
Bucknall Collection/Ian Allan Library

Left:
By way of contrast the
replacements for the L&YR
trans-Pennine services are
now operated by the new
Class 158 DMUs. Two of the
class, Nos 158804 and
158904, are seen at York in
early 1992. *Author*

being promoted through the hills at nearby
Standedge and Woodhead. Constructing the
M&L was hard, difficult work, with thousands
of navvies labouring to carve the railway
through inhospitable country; tunnels,
bridges, viaducts, embankments and cuttings
were all created, and dozens of labourers died
in the process.

When the line opened in 1841, it was only
the beginning of what was to become one of
the northern region's most important means
of communication. The story of how the railway developed to service the needs of local
industry and commerce is a lengthy one, and
it has already been adequately told in John
Marshall's excellent trilogy *The Lancashire &
Yorkshire Railway* (David & Charles). Suffice it
to say, that by the late 19th century the
L&YR had grown to such an extent, that it
served almost every major town in the industrial north, and those towns where it did not
have its own stations were served by joint
lines or through carriages

Yet it was not all success, for in its desire to
cater for business traffic the L&YR soon
found itself at the centre of justifiable criticism. By the mid-Victorian era it had earned
the title of 'the most degenerate railway in
the Kingdom', for its services, locomotives
and rolling-stock left a great deal to be
desired. This was particularly so in passenger
traffic, and by this negligence they left the
door open for their competitors to make further inroads into what had been exclusive
L&YR territory. In many ways they had
become a victim of their own success, and in
some regards they appeared to adopt a 'take
it or leave it attitude'. Only the most staid
developments were noticed in certain fields,
and passenger comforts were certainly not

Right:

The real work-horses of the Aspinall period were the 2-4-2 radial tank engines. These gutsy locos performed a wide ranging series of duties which varied from the humble pick up goods to main line express workings. In **1906** No **842** is seen on the L&YR turntable at Skipton (well inside Midland territory) after bringing a train through from Burnley. Just one year old when it was 'captured' by photographer J. H. Wright, No **842** would last into BR days before being withdrawn in May **1948.**
Ian Allan Library

Centre right:

The development of the L&YR steam railmotors is told in chapter five, so at this stage it is sufficient to say that these attractive little sets provided a very valuable service on a number of lightly-used lines all over the L&YR system. By providing retractable steps on the trailer coaches new halts could be built at sleeper level, thus providing more stops without the considerable expense of building a new station. Towards the end of its days No **10600** is seen at Horwich Works in March **1947** — it was to be cut up just a few weeks later.
J Davenport

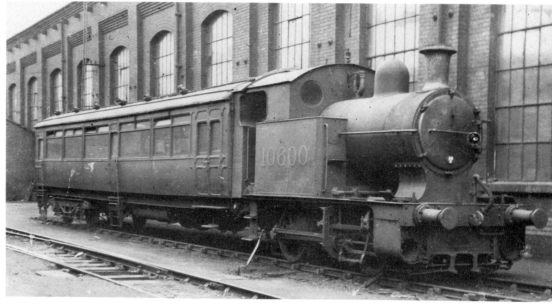

Below right:

As the L&YR classes began finally to disappear in the late 1950s and early 1960s, many saw their last days being eked out with lowly shunting duties and goods turns, but a few were destined for one final round of stardom. A number of enthusiasts' rail tours around the region saw special requests for certain ex-L&YR types as the motive power, including this four-coach tour seen at Chadderton Goods in September 1960, with 2-4-2T No **50850** at the front and 0-6-0 No **52271** at the rear.
J. Davenport

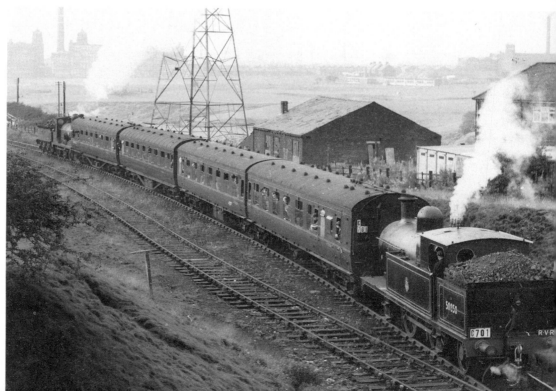

given a high priority. Huge profits were being made from the carriage of freight traffic, and on most workmen's trains the occupants would presumably give little thought to the need for luxurious accommodation in their carriage. Rough, functional and dour are probably good descriptions of L&YR trains, yet before the end of the century this was all to change.

The first major improvements were made by William Barton Wright who, on his appointment as the Chief Mechanical Engineer in 1876, inherited a very disparate situation. In many accounts on the L&YR, Barton Wright is pictured as a lack-lustre character not possessing any great qualities. Such a view is rather unfair, for he slowly began a programme of standardisation. Where possible he rebuilt existing locomotives, though to fill the shortfall in motive power he purchased locomotives from outside sources like the Stirling 'GNR' 0-4-2 tender engines ordered

from Sharp Stewart. As far as the L&YR classes were concerned, he had standardised on just four basic types by the time of his resignation, these being the 0-6-0 tender goods, the 6ft 4-4-0s, and two types of 0-6-2 tank engine, one for goods and one for passenger work.

Following the departure of Barton Wright in 1886, John A. F. Aspinall was appointed as CME and an extensive building programme was instituted. His approach was more radical and, perhaps, his most significant contribution was the development of a class of radial tank engines for both local and express work. The design was so successful that over 300 of these ubiquitous 2-4-2Ts were built, and for over 50 years they were synonymous with the intensive suburban workings that typified the L&YR system. There was also an acute shortage of large express locomotives which Aspinall had to address, and thus began his development of a highly successful class of

Above:
With a number of BR engines being built at Horwich, the new standard types were no strangers to the ex-L&YR system. The introduction of these Standards was heralded with great enthusiasm by the 'spotters', but they soon became commonplace, and were to be seen performing all manner of duties. In June 1952 Standard Class 5 4-6-0 No 73028 is seen on a Blackpool-Manchester working passing Lostock Junction.
J. Davenport

Below left:
As the year of 1968 drew on, the ex-L&YR sheds of North Lancashire came to be among the last strongholds of steam. One such shed was Rose Grove, where steam remained to the bitter end — yet three months before its demise, it is two English Electric Type 4s, (TOPS Class 40), Nos D216/D223, that are to haul the Royal Train through Rose Grove station after the Queen had boarded it at Burnley Central.
D. Bradley

Right:

Quite what the future holds for BR is open to conjecture, and it can be honestly stated that the railways have been starved of adequate funding by governments of all political shades for the past 40 years. However, in recent years the concept of a public railway service has changed out of all recognition from what was known in L&YR days. Freight traffic has virtually vanished off many lines, though passenger services seem to have been stabilised at their current levels. Meanwhile a taste of an electrified future is seen at Blackpool North in September 1991, with driving unit No 82151 at the head of a departure for London Euston. However, until long term investment is provided to electrify the line to Blackpool, trains on the section down to Preston remain strictly diesel-powered.
Martin Eltham

Below right:

While freight has virtually disappeared from much of the former L&YR area, a number of lines have shown a specific increase in recent years. This picture illustrates the type of traffic originating off the Preston Docks branch, a line which leaves the West Coast main line just south of the town at Preston South Junction. It then descends through Fishergate Tunnel to the Port of Preston Authority Exchange Sidings. On 30 March 1989 a pair of Class 31s (Nos 31154 and 31207) leave the exchange sidings with 7Z60 the 08.53 to Lindsey with a train of empty oil/bitumen tankers.
Paul D. Shannon

4-4-0 tender engines. This was followed by the more powerful '1400' class 4-4-2s which, when built, carried the largest boilers fitted to any locomotive in Britain. In the field of goods traffic he further developed the 0-6-0 tender engines and introduced an eight-wheeled coupled type, thereby providing locomotives large enough to meet the ever increasing demands of the traffic department. When Aspinall handed over the reins of office to H. A. Hoy in 1899, the L&YR was an efficient, well run concern. At Horwich it had one of the most modern railway workshops in the country, run by efficient managers and staffed by well-trained engineers.

In addition to the intensive local passenger services, crack express trains ran to very sharp timings between all the principal centres of population. For the more affluent business community, 'club' trains ran an exclusive 'commuter' service from the resort towns into the major cities every morning and back

again in the early evening. The L&YR were also keen to expand commuter facilities for the masses, and regular services ran into Manchester from the city's northern suburbs. Liverpool was similarly served by an 'out of town' workforce who saw the attraction of settling in the communities along the coast towards Southport. Not only did the L&YR make an active attempt to promote such traffic through advertising the benefits of 'suburbia', they also provided the services to go with it. For example, they were one of the first English railways to introduce rapid transit schemes based on electric traction. With this new forward-thinking policy, when the L&YR entered the 20th century, it was well on its way to having an enviable reputation.

In 1904 George Hughes, arguably one of the company's finest engineers, was appointed as CME. He steered the L&YR through the boom years of the Edwardian era, and then took them through the difficult years of

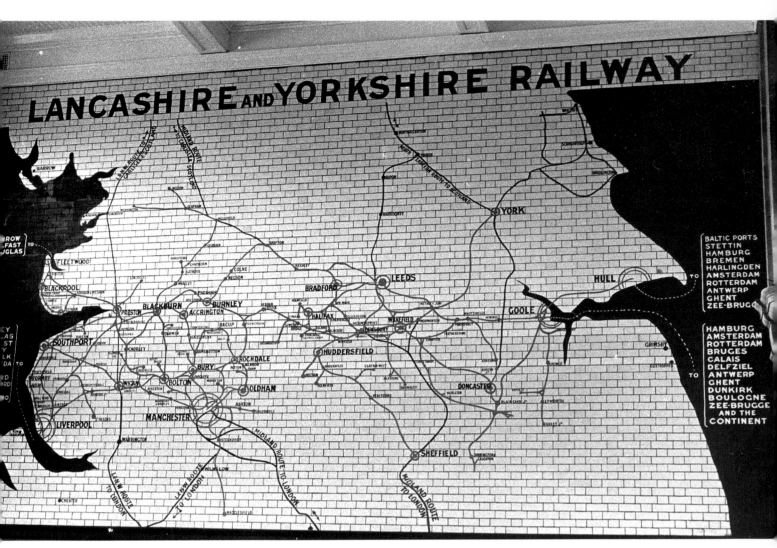

World War 1 between 1914 and 1919. The L&YR played an important role in the movement of vital war traffic and a large portion of its workshop capacity was turned over to essential war-manufactures, whilst its London office became an important annexe of the Railway Executive Committee. Unfortunately, like the majority of private railway companies, the hard war years dealt a severe blow to the L&YR. Little money had been available for normal repair and replacement work, and even essential maintenance had been deferred. The Executive realised that the days of the private railway companies were past, and legislation was obtained for the Government to group many of the 147 concerns into just four companies.

As a prelude to the Grouping it was decided that the L&YR would merge with the London & North Western Railway, a year ahead of the other amalgamations. From 1 January 1922 its massive capital of £72,321,930 was added to that of its former rivals, thus creating one of the largest stock companies of the day. Significantly, when the London Midland & Scottish Railway was formed in 1923, L&YR men occupied the most important positions in the new concern and it was Hughes who became the LMS's first CME.

In the years that followed there have been several major closures, many of which were accelerated by the Beeching Report of the 1960s. The most notable losses are the West Lancashire Railway, the Axholme Joint line and the Spen Valley line, along with the demise of major stations like Liverpool Exchange, Bradford Exchange and Blackpool Central. However, the fact that so many lines are still extant, makes the L&YR unique when it is compared with many of its pre-Grouping contemporaries. Yet, despite the size and complexity of the L&YR network, it is perhaps less well known than its neighbours and rivals. It had no pretensions of being anything but a local line, serving local people, it never had a terminus in London, and it settled for a no-nonsense attitude which concentrated on capturing the ample business traffic of the industrial north. Little wonder that the Lancashire & Yorkshire Railway styled itself as 'the Business-line'; though for many it was, and will always be known simply as 'the *Lanky*'.

Above:
A reminder, before examining the various parts of the L&YR network, of the extent of the company's operations before 1922. This superb map still remains one of the more dramatic features of Manchester Victoria station. *R. G. Fox*

13

1

The Main Line through Lancashire

Genesis

When the M&L began running over the Pennines, its pioneering approach to traversing rough terrain took railways into a new field of operation. This bold venture had first been proposed as early as 1825, but it was not until November 1830 that George Stephenson's survey was published. Even then the proposals were fiercely resisted by various bodies (principally the Rochdale Canal Company, who displayed determined opposition to the proposed railway). They fought the M&L through Parliament for over five years, claiming the canal could deliver goods from Manchester to Halifax (32 miles), in 20 hours at the rate of 2d per ton per mile. They dismissed speed as an irrelevant factor, pointing out that half of its income came from the carriage of grain, which required storage in their warehouses once it arrived at its destination anyway. The M&L retorted, that if this was so, they had nothing to fear from the coming of the railway which could complete the same journey in two to three hours.

In face of all the contradictory evidence the M&L's first bill was thrown out, and a long bitter period followed with argument and counter-argument being submitted, delaying the passage of the Bill's successor. As pro-railway factions argued with the 'traditionalists', the passage of the Bill slowed down even more and the matter became a costly business

for both parties. Eventually the Bill received Royal Assent in July 1836, and a difficult tactical campaign then turned into a difficult constructional one. Some five years were to elapse before the opening of the through route could be considered, though some sections did open earlier. By 1841 the line was complete and the engineers could rightfully express satisfaction in their work. However, travel over the route was not the most pleasant experience with open carriages, smoky tunnels, spark-emitting locomotives and above all the Pennine weather to contend with. Even so, the M&L was well patronised and it settled down to a period of steady progress through the months and years which followed services gradually improved, branch lines were built and an ever widening corridor of countryside was served by the railway.

Manchester Victoria

It would appear that the most logical place to begin any description of the M&L, or the L&YR for that matter, is Manchester's Victoria station for it was long the headquarters of the railway. Yet this was not the original Manchester terminus of the M&L, for that was initially situated in Oldham Road. However, even before the M&L opened, the inadequacies of that terminus were clearly realised by the directors. As a consequence it was decided that a connecting link should be built

Below:

The first selection of photographs illustrates the four ages of rail travel on the L&YR main line, commencing with this fine study of No 1403, an Aspinall 4-4-2 Atlantic, on an eastbound express. The date is sometime in the first two years of the present century, and the location Sowerby Bridge — notice the train communication cord stretching over the tender to the cab roof!

Real Photographs/Ian Allan Library

14

with the Liverpool & Manchester's terminus in Liverpool Road, but at this stage the value of through rail routes had not yet been fully appreciated and there was little enthusiasm for co-operation. Yet, in July 1838, when a through route from Liverpool to Hull became a realistic objective, a preliminary agreement was reached by the two companies. A connection was thus projected from the M&L, near Miles Platting, to Hunt's Bank, with a new 'inter-change station' to be completed as and when the L&M and Manchester & Bolton railways brought in connections from their lines.

The line opened from Miles Platting to Hunt's Bank on New Year's Day 1844, but at first the L&M were reluctant to build their section. The opening of the new station allowed the simultaneous withdrawal of M&L passenger trains to Oldham Road, and the original terminal became a goods depot. By the kind permission of Her Majesty Queen Victoria, the new single-platform station bore the ruling monarch's name. The accommodation may sound inadequate, but the solitary platform was no less than 852 feet long. In due course the L&M built their link line, and thereafter Leeds trains used the eastern end

Above:
Moving into the LMS era, we find a profusion of L&YR types being retained, particularly the 0-6-0 tender engines and the 2-4-2 tanks, many of which lasted well into BR days. Preparing for its next stint of duty from Agecroft shed is No 12301 (formerly L&YR No 417) built in September 1895 and withdrawn in May 1938 — of interest is the tender which was originally fitted to one of 6ft 4-4-0s of 1885-86.
Author's Collection

Left:
Ex-L&YR 0-6-0 No 52271 lasted considerably longer than its sister pictured previously, and it is seen at Manchester Victoria East Junction in 1959 waiting to assist a preceding goods train up Miles Platting Incline — apart from the livery changes, this view could almost have been taken any time in the previous half-century.
J. Davenport

Right:
One of the most significant improvements around Manchester in recent years has been the Windsor Link. Though this was only originally envisaged as an operating line between the city's two main railway routes, it has proved to be an ideal means of linking the passenger services between the city's two main stations. With the provision of a new interchange station at Salford Crescent the scheme has proven to be perfectly viable and, as a result, the platform facilities at Crescent are already in need of enlargement. On 3 June 1991 No 37430 heads towards the station with the five-coach 17.06 Manchester Victoria-Southport service.
Paul D. Shannon

Below right:
Before the construction of Victoria station, the M&L had to be content with a rather inadequate terminus in Oldham Road some considerable distance from the city's other railway terminals. When sense prevailed and the joint station was erected at Hunt's Bank, Oldham Road became a goods depot but its cramped location needed numerous wagon turntables to permit reasonable operation. Still bearing the inscription Manchester & Leeds Railway the station is pictured in 1963 prior to the final run down and closure.
British Railways (LMR)

Far right:
Victoria station had a far more impressive air about it than Oldham Road, and after successive improvement schemes it became a symbol of the city's prosperity. Despite years of grime, neglect, and even attacks by the German Luftwaffe, it still has a magnificent air of dignity as pictured in February 1991, on the day of the M&L's 150th anniversary.
Martin Eltham

and Liverpool trains the western. The Bolton trains however did not use the station at first, and these continued to terminate in Salford.

As the M&L line climbed out of Victoria, the bank up to Oldham Road Junction was quite severe with gradients as steep as 1 in 47. As locomotives of the day were not capable of hauling any but the smallest of trains up the incline, a stationary winding engine, with an interesting method of operation, was installed at Miles Platting. A break-van (*sic*) attached to a wire rope was coupled to the front of ascending locomotives and the train would thus be assisted to the summit; as trains descended the bank gravity had a tendency to overcome the inadequate brakes of that time, so the van and the wire rope would be attached at the back of the train to prevent runaways. Fortunately locomotive performance and braking quickly improved, and it would appear that the winding engine operations were discontinued as early as 1845.

From 1846 a gradually increasing number of the Bolton trains ran into Victoria, and the anomaly was finally resolved when the M&B merged into the M&L. With three railways now using Victoria, the pressure on the single platform became intense, and a series of station improvements were to follow. At an early stage a bay was added at each end of the platform, but this did not relieve the congestion which was beginning to build up at peak times. In 1855 a set of suburban platforms were built on the south side of the main plat-

form, providing facilities to accommodate trains from Oldham and Stalybridge. Two more main line platforms were erected in the mid-1860s, but these were short-lived and replaced about 10 years later when the first major rebuilding took place. When this programme was completed in 1884 it provided the station with five bays and six through platforms. These were made up as follows: four bay platforms in the suburban section, the original platform, two curved islands, and a platform with a through line and a east-facing bay at the far side of the station. A product of this development was the transfer of the remaining LNWR trains from Victoria to Exchange.

In the latter years of the 19th century, station improvements were instituted again. A novel feature of this period was the little electric overhead railway installed by J. A. F. Aspinall, in 1899, for the conveyance of luggage and parcels in a basket-work 'skip'. The overhead railway was suspended from the roof and therefore carried high above the platforms and running lines, thereby reducing the need for porters to convey items over barrow crossings or through the subways. When the railway reached the required platform, the 'skip' was simply lowered to the ground for emptying or loading and then raised back up to the operating height. By 1903 the station had been fully rebuilt, with the number of bays increasing to 11. Some seven years after the Grouping, Victoria's original plat-

Above:
Victoria station was divided into two distinct sections: the through platforms and the suburban bays. The bays were at the eastern end, and waiting to leave that side of the station is Agecroft shed's No 744 a Hoy 2-6-2 side tank built in February 1904. It is seen probably shortly after that date with a working for Oldham. In theory these immensely powerful engines were a good idea for the work they had to undertake, but a rigid wheelbase and problems with cracked main-frames led to their relegation to banking duties around the period 1913-16. Withdrawals began in 1920 and No 744 was the last to go in August 1926.
Bucknall Collection/Ian Allan Library

17

Right:
'Black 5' No 45203 acts as station pilot at Manchester Victoria station on 1 June 1968. Latterly the bay platforms at Victoria became the preserve of the Bury line service and of the many parcels trains that originated at the station. *R. W. Courtney*

Below right:
Waiting in one of the surviving bay platforms at Manchester Victoria is Class 142 No 142051. Under the modernisation scheme, only two bay platforms in Victoria's suburban section will be retained, along with the 1844 platform. The through island platforms will see major improvements, and these will be completely rebuilt to form just four through platforms, roughly equivalent to today's platforms Nos 11-14. In the rebuilding, opportunity should be taken to straighten out the twisting S-curves which are a legacy of the original Hunt's Bank connections with the B&P. It is also intended to remove the long subway and replace it with a new footbridge from platform No 11. Much of the modernisation scheme for the suburban platforms was the result of the Metrolink project and one of the new Metrolink cars, No 1005, can be seen on the extreme left of the picture. Metrolink trams heading for Piccadilly take a sharp left bend in the station and head out into the streets of the city through a new exit.
Author

form of 1844, No 11, was extended to join platform No 3 in the ex-LNWR Exchange station. This resulted in the creation of the world's longest platform — and a sign was duly erected to proclaim that it was no less than 2,238ft long.

Travellers passing through Victoria today will notice that it has a woeful look in parts, and may be tempted to put this down to the neglect of recent times. Yet, careful investigation will reveal that parts of the once magnificent over-all roof have now been missing for exactly half a century. In December 1941 the German Luftwaffe came to attack Manchester, and a hail of bombs showered down on the city. The railways were prime targets; Victoria and nearby Exchange were no exceptions. The reminders of that attack are still to be found, and until recently a yard lamp standing near Exchange station revealed traces of the scorching it received during the attack. In the postwar years there was not the money for repairs, and in the 1950s and 1960s there simply was not the will.

In 1967 Exchange station closed and trains on the ex-LNWR routes were all concentrated on Victoria. Even so this coincided with the gradual erosion of local services and the use of the ex-L&YR station also declined. The following year the original Oldham Road terminus closed, as freight traffic also declined. The sorry state of affairs appeared as though it could only get worse, but a reprieve was held out in the form of the Picc-Vic line, a new rail route through the city centre with the object of connecting the southern and northern rail networks of Greater Manchester and the city's two principal stations. Regretfully that was eventually ruled out on financial considerations, and thus the decline seemed destined to continue. However, two exciting developments of the

1980s finally provided the answer, these being the Windsor link at the west end of the city and the new Metrolink (discussed in detail later).

The Windsor link came about in an unusual way, because after the demise of Picc-Vic Greater Manchester PTE were anxious to find some other way of revitalising Victoria and the northern rail network. A long standing proposal to electrify the route from Victoria to Blackpool North was resurrected, using a 25kV ac system. One of the problems, however, was where to stable and maintain the electric rolling stock, because to take the wires east of Victoria to a new depot on the north side was considered too expensive. The answer was, in effect, to revive a line partially constructed in 1904 from Wind-

sor Bridge to Ordsall Lane, thereby gaining access for electric trains to the south side 25kV system and the associated depot at Longsight.

However, the marketing people soon latched upon the new idea, because here would be a partial answer to bridging the north/south divide. The opening of a through electric 'Spine' route, Stockport-Piccadilly-Bolton-Blackpool, opened up vast new possibilities for attracting additional passengers. The scheme was developed with enthusiasm and for financial authority was divided into two parts, firstly the construction of the new line, secondly the electrification of the Castlefield Junction-Euxton Junction and Preston No 5 (Fylde) Junction-Blackpool North sections. Perversely, the former was approved,

Above left:
One of the features of Victoria is the station concourse with its bookstalls and restaurants. In the pre-Nationalisation era, W. H. Smith's shop proudly promotes reading as the source of all knowledge and the LMS takes advantage of its own station to advertise travel and hotels.
B. C. Lane Collection

Left:
More than half a century later W. H. Smith has modernised its bookstall, although the ornate lettering above remains intact, and the prime advertising location is no longer the preserve of the railway.
Author

Right:
The line adjacent to the through platforms at Victoria was regularly used for the stabling of pilot engines. On 23 June 1967 'Black 5' No 45076 fulfils the station pilot duty, whilst one of the trans-Pennine DMU sets forms the 8.43am departure towards Leeds running 15min late. The trans-Pennine sets are now as much a part of history as the steam trains they replaced.
G. N. G. Tingey

Below:
The through road at Victoria is still used for the stabling of locomotives as evidenced by this 16 February 1992 illustration. Class 31 No 31144, in the so-called 'Dutch' livery, awaits its next turn in the company of an InterCity liveried Class 37/4.
Author

the latter rejected and the consequent operating problems have proved a considerable disadvantage to this day, but the scheme has again been revived and is on the Priority list of the PTE. A new island station, Salford Crescent, was opened in 1987, and the two platform faces provide easy interchange between Victoria and Piccadilly services. The success of the new station had an effect on the existing station at Salford, which has become something of an eyesore today. Even so it is well patronised at peak times.

Piccadilly was thus becoming the main focal point for through trains, with the main trans-Pennine services now being diverted from Stalybridge via Guide Bridge to Piccadilly and regaining the Chat Moss route at Ordsall Lane, but not actually using the Windsor Link. Many other local services which previously terminated at Victoria or Piccadilly became trains passing through and beyond Manchester thus providing several new passenger links. Some of the trains from Huddersfield (or beyond) continue to use Victoria, as does service over the Calder Valley route from Yorkshire which has been increased in frequency, some running through to Liverpool as of old but to Lime Street in place of Exchange. Meanwhile services to North Wales (mainly ex-LNWR destinations) continue to use the station, and thus it has enjoyed something of a minor revival.

To the east side of the station a major rationalisation has gone ahead; partly influenced by Metrolink, and partly by the reduction in the number of services due to the re-routing via Piccadilly. The Cheetham Hill line from Victoria East Junction, which the L&YR built with easier gradients as a means to reach Thorpes Bridge Junction, is now pri-

marily used for freight traffic. The original incline of 1844 is timetabled to carry the bulk of all services going east from Victoria, despite its severe gradient. Meanwhile the former L&YR line to Bury, which runs parallel with the old M&L for a short while before tunnelling below it at Collyhurst, has been converted to carry Manchester's new light railway system - Metrolink. At the time of writing a considerable amount of work is going on at Victoria in connection with Metrolink, and one assumes that this will occupy much of the PTE's time and resources in the immediate future. Two Metrolink platforms providing three faces have been installed in the old suburban section, thus providing sufficient capacity for extra trains should the Oldham-Rochdale phase of the system go ahead. However, once the current work is completed and finances become available, a major refurbishment is planned for Victoria.

North From Manchester

From the top of the incline the line curves north-east through a station at Miles Platting, though this was substantially altered to a junction station after the Stalybridge branch opened in 1846. At Thorpes Bridge the M&L line was joined by the four track Cheetham Hill route from Manchester Victoria, which was authorised in the 1870s having been conceived as a means of relieving pressure on the incline - particularly since this was also being used by LNWR trains to Leeds. Construction of the two-mile long line was not difficult, but it involved a considerable section of elevated track-work and viaducts. A junction was made with the Bury line at Cheetham Hill, and carriage sidings were provided at Red

Above:

Though the Miles Platting-avoiding line was the main route for most through trains, its future is now in some doubt. The carriage sidings at Red Bank and Queen's Road have already closed, and though BR are keeping the line open to avoid banking heavy trains up to Miles Platting, it might be considered as something of a luxury. In the latter days of steam, however, it was still an immensely important facility, containing four important carriage stabling areas. On 15 May 1964, the now preserved No 45596 *Bahamas* marshals an ECS train past Cheetham Hill sidings before taking it to Victoria where it will form a train to Blackpool.
R S Greenwood

The scene at the Victoria end of Miles Platting bank on 14 February 1989, as No 37065 approaches the station with the daily Ashburys-Warrington Speedlink trip working. The load includes engineers' wagons from Castleton; a new hopper wagon from Heywood wagon works; and empty ferry vans and carbon dioxide tanks from Ardwick West freight depot. Sadly Speedlink is firmly relegated to the 'then' category, the service having now been withdrawn by BR.
Paul D. Shannon

Bank and Queens Road on the Miles Platting-avoiding line. The latter carriage sidings being the day-time home for the ex-LMS articulated 'Coronation Scot' sets which were used on the Blackpool Club trains for some years. The carriage sidings at Red Bank, Queens Road (now the home of the new Metrolink depot) and Cheetham Hill have all closed, together with the Lightbowne sidings situated opposite Newton Heath depot.

The opening of the 'avoiding' line in 1877 coincided closely with the decision to move the L&YR's main locomotive facilities from Miles Platting. The original M&L locomotive shed at this site suffered from being in a restricted position alongside the main line, which was also the location of the company's locomotive manufacturing plant. Such a restricted site was not conducive either to good operating conditions or manufacturing, and a gradual transfer of these facilities began. The 150-engine shed that opened at Newton Heath in 1876 was the first of these changes, and they culminated with the removal of the loco-manufacturing/repair capacity to a purpose built works near Bolton in 1887. Carriage and wagon production was centred on Newton Heath, and during the 1914-18 period the works there carried out invaluable war work — including the construction of several ambulance trains.

Newton Heath shed was a massive affair based on an LNWR design, and at the height of its development it occupied the whole of the triangular area formed by the main line, the new Oldham branch, and Dean Lane. When steam locomotives were withdrawn from the shed in 1968, the site was redeveloped around 1970 as a diesel depot incorporating DMU cleaning facilities. This role is maintained today, with further facilities being added after a major refurbishment in the mid-1980s. There was a passenger station at Newton Heath, but this closed in January 1966, and thereafter passengers had to make do with the nearby Dean Lane station on the Oldham line. This branch had opened from a junction near Newton Heath in 1880 as an alternative to the Werneth Incline, the original M&L route to Oldham.

North of Newton Heath the main line continued on through Moston, where a station was erected in 1872 to meet the growing level of commuter traffic to Manchester. The line then reached a point near Middleton where, in 1842, a station was erected to serve as junction for the M&L branch to Oldham. This line took just eight months to build, but it involved the notorious Werneth Incline. This was a ¾ mile long bank with a gradient of 1 in 27, and was rope-worked from the opening for a period of around 10 years. In 1852 the station on the main line was re-named Middleton Junction, a name which became particularly applicable after a branch opened down into Middleton itself in January 1857. Though this line was not as steeply graded as the Werneth line, it still had sections as severe as 1 in 80. Both of the lines which diverged from the M&L at Middleton Junction suffered badly in the postwar period, despite the introduction of two-car DMUs in 1958. Werneth Incline closed to passenger trains in 1960 and the branch to Middleton lost its service in 1964 followed by the withdrawal of goods trains one year later.

Above:
Fairburn-designed 2-6-4T No 42289 on a Middleton-Manchester Victoria service departs from Middleton Junction in July 1952.
J. Davenport

Left:
Thirty-four years later, on 8 March 1986, Class 142 No 142013, in the orange and brown livery of Greater Manchester PTE, heads past Middleton West Junction with a train from Rochdale to Victoria. Although the signalbox and gantry remain intact from the earlier scene, Middleton station has completely disappeared.
Paul D. Shannon

Left:
Manchester was served by two large L&YR engine sheds, Agecroft and Newton Heath. The later was of such a size that no less than 24 roads passed through the shed, but as steam was withdrawn from the northwest in the summer of 1968, one of the last bastions of the coal-fired locomotive handed over its allocation to the scrapmen in July. The shed has long since been removed, but this classic view illustrates its importance in L&YR days.
B C Lane Collection

Above:
Class 2MT 2-6-0 No 46439 prepares to remove the DMU forming the 5.35pm Manchester Victoria-Halifax train from the platform at Castleton on 27 May 1964 after the DMU had been on fire.
R. S. Greenwood

Right:
Following the closure of Newton Heath and Middleton Junction stations in 1966, the main line north of Manchester was left with few intermediate stations to serve the suburbs. In 1985 a new station was provided at Mills Hill, but even so there are only three other stations between Manchester and Rochdale — Miles Platting, Moston, and Castleton — and of these Miles Platting is a candidate for early closure. Taken from platform level and looking towards the bridge from which the last photograph was shot, Castleton is pictured on 24 May 1986 as No 56104 powers the 05.45 Fiddlers Ferry-Healey Mills MGR empties. The station retains a number of L&YR features, most notably the station buildings and canopy on the westbound platform. Those on the eastbound platform have, however, been replaced by more basic facilities.
Paul D. Shannon

Rochdale

When the M&L opened its line through Rochdale on 4 July 1839, it significantly increased the prosperity of the town. The canal had been instrumental in opening up industrial development, but it was the railway that was to make the most of it. The countryside around Rochdale is dominated by the Pennine hills and a number of deep valleys which, with their swift flowing water courses, were ideal for the developing textile industry. It was this countryside that the railway could ideally serve, and at an early stage branch lines were being considered to outlying districts.

The first of these lines to be built was to Heywood, and it is interesting to note that it was under construction at the same time as the main line between Littleborough and Hebden Bridge. Opening came on 15 April 1841 just six weeks after the through line, which it left by a junction at Blue Pits (Castleton). Little is known about its construction, as it was built by 'way-leaves' (without Act of Parliament). However, its early period of operation is of considerable interest as it was worked entirely by horses for about six years. The second stage of its development is more closely associated with the Liverpool & Bury Railway which was authorised in 1847,

Above left:
With three branches — Heywood, Oldham and Bacup — Rochdale became an important railway centre at a very early stage. By the end of the 19th century its station was rebuilt with four main line platform faces and several bays. On 28 September 1956 'Compound' 4-4-0 No 41193 pauses with an excursion to Blackpool whilst No 4 bay is being used to stage a special railway exhibition to mark Rochdale's centenary. The bay is occupied by an 'EM2' class electric locomotive, a cafeteria car, a new BR Standard 4MT 4-6-0 and ex-Furness Railway *Copper Nob*. On opening the exhibition the Mayor of Rochdale commented, 'What would the life of our town be like if the railway ceased to function?'. Fortunately it still survives!
H. Wells

Left:
Though the railway lives on, the town's station is an incongruous mix between old and new, with the modern buildings contrasting sharply with three decaying yellow brick buildings at the western end of the remaining platform. At the eastern end of this 'island' a single track runs into the sole remaining bay, which serves as a terminus for trains traversing the Oldham loop. On 27 September 1991 a West Yorkshire Metro Class 158 DMU, No 158908, the 09.46 from York to Manchester, waits in platform.
Michael Eltham

to make an end-on junction with the M&L at Heywood. The opening of this line at the end of 1848 not only provided a through route to Rochdale from Liverpool, Wigan, Bolton and Bury but, by the construction of a new south-facing curve at Blue Pits, it also gave another route into Manchester.

During the 1850s the Oldham, Ashton & Guide Bridge Junction Railway was promoted to construct a useful link between three railway systems to the east of Manchester, a scheme supported by the LNWR, L&YR and MS&LR. However, before the line from Guide Bridge was complete, the L&YR dropped out of the coalition. This left the OA&GBJR viewing the possibility of extending their line through to Bacup via Rochdale and the Whitworth Valley. However, the L&YR acted swiftly and in August 1859 they received Parliamentary sanction to construct a line from Rochdale to Oldham Mumps, and to forestall any further encroachment into its territory, the L&YR pursued their original proposals of extending their line to Bacup.

The M&L had obtained powers to build their branch as early as 1846, but they had done nothing about it. Accordingly the East Lancashire Railway's branch from Bury was the first to reach Bacup in 1852. Though the district was then served by the ELR, when the L&YR opened to Facit in the autumn of 1870 it was the first stage in their attempt to reach a rich source of industrial traffic. Surprisingly the L&YR failed to make any real progress, and the line was not opened through to Bacup until 1 December 1881. This was the final stage in the development of Rochdale's railway network, but the ever increasing importance of the town's station as a major junction continued. The original station at the east side of Oldham Road was soon found to be inadequate, and was considerably enlarged in the years which followed. The station was completely rebuilt in 1892 with two large islands, the one on the Up lines had two bay platforms at the west end, whilst the Down side's bays were at the east.

The first major casualty of the area was the LMS's withdrawal of the lightly-used passenger trains to Bacup just five months before nationalisation. The goods service was retained however, and it lasted another 19½ years finally ceasing at the end of 1966. North of Rochdale the small station on the main line at Smithy Bridge which had opened in 1868 closed completely in 1960, just failing to make its centenary. Today, support from the local Passenger Transport Authority led to its reinstatement with a pair of timber-built platforms being erected and the station came back into service when the Summit Tunnel re-opening took place. However, the new station no longer straddles the level crossing as before, but has both platforms on the Manchester side.

Goods services on the line from Rochdale to Bury were withdrawn during the mid-1960s, but the passenger service to Bolton remained intact until October 1970. Though the DMUs operating passenger services on this vital cross-country route had been poorly patronised for some time, they were at an unfair disadvantage to the better subsidised bus routes. If the line had managed to remain in operation a little longer, the Greater Manchester PTE would probably have been able to offer a subsidy to ensure its survival. The line became goods-only, serving the coal concentration depot at Rawtenstall but eventually closed in December 1980, when it was cut back as far as Heywood. However, a renaissance may be in store, as the East Lancashire Railway will be extending their line through to Heywood in the future; meanwhile, the BR Civil Engineering Depot at Castleton and Powell-Duffryn continue to originate traffic on the branch.

Station 'improvements' at Rochdale began in 1974 when the two storey buildings on the Up island were demolished and the awnings on the Down platforms replaced. In 1979 the Up island was taken out of use, reducing the six remaining platforms to just three. During the following year a modern entrance lobby, parcels office and booking hall were erected on the Down island platform. In addition to the Manchester trains, a number of services originate from Rochdale which currently continue to Wigan Wallgate via Oldham; others take the direct route to Manchester going forward to Bolton and Blackburn. During the summer months some of the services are extended beyond the boundaries of Greater Manchester, with more distant destinations like Southport and Blackpool being offered.

Summit

To cross the watershed at Summit, a tunnel 2,885yd long was built which, at the time of opening, was the world's longest railway tunnel. Construction of the bore and the approach lines began early in 1838, and the shafts were sunk almost at once despite the atrocious winter weather. The first bricks were laid in one of the shafts in August, and No 10 shaft was finished by November. Unfortunately the work on the main tunnel was quite laborious, and progress was notoriously slow — so in March 1839 the contractors working on the driftways were replaced. Work progressed more rapidly now, but the number of accidents continued apace with several fatalities.

The tunnel was a costly operation in lives, but in those days lives came cheaply, and it was the speed of the project which was paramount. However, the building work was running into trouble in financial terms as well. The initial costs had been estimated by Gooch at £156,000, but even before it was completed this figure had shown a 25%

increase — an expensive jump at the time when the line had still to earn a penny in revenue. Then there was the trouble with the bricklayers in 1840, when the men formed a 'combination' (union) to force improvements in working conditions and pay — the ring leaders were gaoled by Rochdale's magistrates, and the work went ahead with little improvement for the other men. The work they did was quite demanding, laying around 23 million bricks in thicknesses varying from five to 10 rings — in doing so they used 8,000 tons of cement and required 20,000 tons of candles to illuminate their working areas.

On 11 December 1840 the last brick was put in place by Barnard Dickinson, the tunnel engineer, who later said that the tunnel 'would defy the ravages of tempest, fire or war, or wasting of age'. With this work completed the trains from Normanton to Hebden Bridge were extended to the east end of the tunnel, and a stage coach service instituted along the turnpike to Littleborough. With the approval of the Board of Trade the last section of the line opened to traffic on March 1 1841, and M&L trains began running through to Normanton.

Today it is interesting to reflect on the accuracy of Dickinson's claim, as we can prove it was no idle boast. For a century and a half Summit has defied the atrocious Pennine weather, safely passed through two world wars, and withstood one of the world's worst subterranean railway fires. This conflagration began on 20 December 1984, after a train of oil tankers became derailed and then caught fire inside the bore. The blaze raged for several days, and despite determined efforts by the West Yorkshire Fire Service, flames roared out of the tunnel portals and belched skywards from the ventilation shafts. When the flames were eventually extinguished, and fire-brigade officials allowed BR engineers inside, it was feared that the tunnel would be irreparably damaged — but it was not. The subsequent inspection proved George Stephenson right, for on its opening he said that 'he would stake his head and character upon it'. His reputation unsullied, the tunnel reopened, after repairs, on Monday 19 August 1985 when a Greater Manchester liveried DMU, No 142001, was the 'first' train through followed immediately thereafter by a Class 141 in West Yorkshire livery.

Above:
The first trains ran to Littleborough on 3 July 1838, when the station became a terminus of the first M&L services from Manchester. It has never been a busy station, but its level of patronage has always been above average for what might be anticipated from an equivalent station. In the early part of the present century an unidentified Aspinall 4-4-2 heads a lightweight three-coach train towards Littleborough, obviously during the summer months — a fact testified to by the hay-drying posts and wires in the field above the loco's front buffer beam.
B. C. Lane Collection

2

The Main Line Through Yorkshire

Todmorden

Todmorden has long been a staging point on the route between Yorkshire and Lancashire, and its railway development reflects this centuries-old tradition. Indeed, when it opened, Todmorden was advertised as the station for Burnley. Though this might seem an extravagant claim, we must remember that in the 1840s a gap of just 10 miles or so was neither here nor there. So despite the fact that a horse-bus service had to negotiate the difficult Cliviger Gorge, Todmorden was soon handling a considerable number of passengers for north Lancashire. Because of various difficulties a pair of wooden platforms were in use up to 1843-44, when the plans for a permanent station were implemented. Unfortunately, by the time the stone station was built at the end of the viaduct, it was already too small for the traffic it was handling, so new plans were drawn up and in 1865 the present station was built. However, even this was found to be inadequate, and during the late 19th century it was substantially enlarged.

The importance of Todmorden increased when the M&L's 'branch' line to Burnley, via the Cliviger Gorge, opened to traffic. The work on this line had been authorised in 1845, and, though construction began shortly afterwards, financial difficulties and the severe winter of 1847-48 forced the abandonment of the work for a short while. The summit of the line at Copy Pit was 749ft above sea level, so it was not surprising that the weather should have such a marked effect on the work. Yet, once resumed, construction proceeded quickly and by the autumn of 1849 a single line of rails had reached Burnley allowing the line to open in November. The following year a connection was made with the East Lancashire Railway at Gannow near Rose Grove, providing a direct route from Yorkshire to north Lancashire.

In 1860 the branch line was eventually doubled throughout, but passenger trains from the east had to draw into Todmorden station and then reverse before continuing to Burnley. In 1862 this operating anomaly was resolved by the construction of a curve between Hall Royd and Stansfield Hall, where junctions were made with the existing lines. Yet this large triangular junction did not completely resolve the problem, as trains running from Yorkshire to towns in north Lancashire now had to miss out Todmorden.

In order to prevent this, and thereby avoid losing much-needed custom, the L&YR opened a station at Stansfield Hall (for Todmorden) in 1869.

Passenger services along the route were always well patronised, particularly those through trains making for the Lancashire coastal resorts. Several express trains were routed this way, but few passed over Copy Pit in the winter months. Local stations on the route did not last long, and those at Holme and Cornholme closed in 1930 and 1938 respectively. In July 1944 Stansfield Hall station was closed by the LMS, a decision largely influenced by the wartime conditions then prevailing. Townley was the next to go in 1952, though goods traffic lingered on until 1960. Portsmouth went in 1958 with the goods service being withdrawn just five year's later. What was advertised as a Todmorden-Rose Grove local service remained in operation, but the value of this has to be questioned because of the absence of intermediate stations and the closure of Burnley's Manchester Road station in 1961. However, the service did provided a useful connection for passengers wanting to head to Blackpool and it remained reasonably well used during the summer months. The winter was another matter, and the average loadings were such that they ensured that it fell victim to the savage cuts in provincial rail services during 1965. After this the Todmorden-Stansfield Hall curve fell into disuse, and was only traversed by the occasional freight train until it was lifted.

In 1984 a DMU service of six trains daily was introduced between Leeds and Preston via Copy Pit, with some of the sets continuing through to Blackpool. That service proved to be of considerable value, particularly as a cross country link from north Lancashire to Yorkshire while Summit Tunnel was closed after the fire. In the 1991-92 winter timetable, there are no less than 11 daily trains from Leeds to Preston — 10 of which continue through to Blackpool North. It is interesting to note that this service grew from a single daily return working between Blackburn and Bradford sponsored as a community service by a building society. Regretfully, there is no longer any way people from Todmorden can catch the Copy Pit trains unless they travel back to Hebden Bridge to board them. This illogical situation has led to

A Southport-Leeds express passes Summit East box headed by Southport-based 'Black 5' No 44729 in charge on **14 June 1961**. *G. W. Morrison*

Left:
The new order on the Calder Valley main line: Class 158 No 158760 heads west towards Lancashire on **3 March 1992**. Apart from the replacement of the semaphore signalling with colour lights and the loss of the traditional telegraph poles, the scene is very much similar to that of 30 years ago.
Author

requests for the Blackpool trains to reverse into the station, but the present track layout and signalling will not permit this. The most suitable answer would be a new junction station at the east end of the town, particularly since the reinstatement of the old curve and a major refurbishment of the station has already been examined and found to be too expensive. East from Todmorden, a small intermediate station once served the village of Eastwood, but this was an early casualty of the nationalised railways — closing to passengers in 1951.

Calder Vale

The section from Hebden Bridge to Normanton opened on Monday 5 October 1840, but as there was no physical connection with the rest of the M&L line, it fell to the North Midland Railway to provide locomotives and stock for the service. The opening was ecstatically welcomed in the locality, but a few of those celebrating the event went a little too far and rode on the carriage roofs of the first train. With all the low bridges and tunnels on the route it is a wonder no-one was killed in

the process. The following month it appeared as though the section to Summit was ready for opening, but various delays prevented this occurrence until New Year's Eve. Hebden Bridge always generated a substantial level of rail traffic, and its station has been well maintained as a result. A particular element of the station's traffic was associated with tourist trade, and in L&YR days the company produced a number of posters proclaiming the virtues of the area, particularly the spectacular countryside around Hardcastle Crags. Today this trend has continued as the town has become something of a successful visitor centre. Located in the heart of the south Pennines, it still has much to offer to excursionists.

Mytholmroyd was reduced to an unstaffed halt in the rationalisation period and most of the buildings were subsequently swept away. In October 1991 a £460,000 improvement programme was completed, with new platforms being erected at one end of the original station. Unfortunately, the new 'bus-shelter' waiting areas can never compare with the roaring waiting room fires which I vividly

Below:
From Summit the line runs down the valley of the Walsden Water, to Walsden station, which is pictured in 1953 and closed to passengers 10 years later. In the autumn of 1990 the West Yorkshire Passenger Transport Executive reopened a basic station conveniently situated for the main street. Like the facility at Smithy Bridge, these modest wooden platforms reflect the growing demand for conveniently situated railway stations and all credit should be paid to the authorities concerned!
David Ibbotson

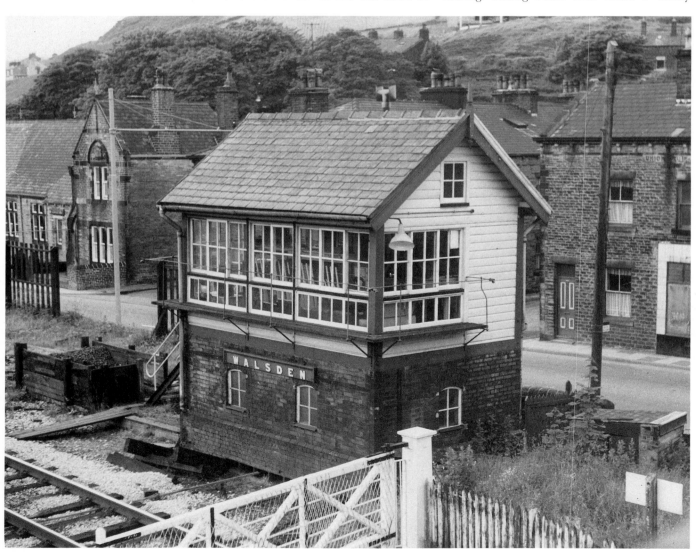

Above:
Todmorden was always an important junction on the L&YR main line, with the Copy Pit route to Burnley diverging at a junction just east of the station. Although the East Lancashire Railway merged with the L&YR in 1859, it was not until 1875 that the ELR's locomotives were numbered in the L&YR series. Carrying its post-1875 number, 0-6-0 No 715 (originally ELR No 115 *Medusa* dating from 1872) is seen at Todmorden station in the late 19th century. Rebuilt in 1897, the locomotive was finally withdrawn in 1900.
B. C. Lane Collection

Above left:
By contrast, Todmorden station of today is little more than a disgrace, its buildings shabby and unkempt, its platforms partially overgrown. The station has been stripped of all but the most basic facilities, although it is still staffed. The course of the once busy line curving round to Stansfield Hall can just be traced in the undergrowth, but there is little else to show what an important junction this once was. In the red and cream livery of West Yorkshire PTA Class 158 No 158903 heads west on 3 March 1992.
Author

recall from my train spotting days. However Mytholmroyd has fared better than its near neighbour, Luddendenfoot, which closed to passengers in 1962, but is now a possible candidate for reopening. The once-vital goods service at these and a number of other local stations ended in 1965.

The western approach to Sowerby Bridge was dominated by the engine shed, which had evolved as a major staging and crew changing point on the route between Lancashire and Yorkshire. The first engine shed dated from 1852 and had once been a carriage shed. Even though it was extended in 1857 the accommodation was not adequate

for the number of locomotives being changed here and in 1887 a new purpose-built shed was opened. After dieselisation the shed's traditional duties, the interminably slow coal trains, could be handled by Type 4 locomotives without the need for banking assistance or crew changing. As a consequence it closed on the first Saturday of 1964, and today what little remains of the shed is used by a road haulage company.

The station is also a shadow of its former self, but it was once a very important junction serving the main line and the branches to Halifax and Rishworth. In August 1840, Bramwell Brontë (brother of the famous nov-

elist sisters) was appointed to the post of assistant clerk in charge at Sowerby Bridge station; the following April he obtained promotion and transferred to Luddendenfoot, but after a sum of £11 went missing he was forced to leave the railway service under something of a cloud. As a prelude to the start of the Rishworth services a new, classical-looking station opened in 1876-79, having been built in the triangle between the main line and the branch. Unfortunately, this branch was an early victim of tram competition, and it closed to passengers six years after the Grouping. Yet goods traffic continued with the need for marshalling at the junction, whilst the station still had an important passenger role to fulfil, particularly from 1962 onwards when most of the services were dieselised and the York trains terminated here to make a connection with the Bradford-Halifax-Manchester workings. It was partially modernised then, but in the years which followed it went into severe decline and many of the buildings were subsequently demolished and today it is another area where the West Yorkshire PTE hope to improve facilities.

Greetland, Elland & Brighouse

Prior to 1844 the section down to Elland was devoid of any stations, but in order to respond to a growing demand for a more convenient interchange for Halifax, a new junction station was opened at North Dean on 1 July 1844. In 1883 it was renamed North Dean and Greetland, correctly reflecting the industrial development in Greetland. The growing town continued to eclipse North Dean, and in the station modernisation scheme of 1897 the station became known solely as Greetland. In 1857 a junction had been created to the west of North Dean sta-

Facing page, top:
Looking along the eastbound platform at Todmorden emphasises how many of the facilities have disappeared, most notably the buildings on this platform and all the station canopies. On 22 May 1988 Class 142 No 142079 forms the 16.05 service to Leeds.
John Bateman

Facing page, bottom:
In the mid-1960s the Copy Pit line became a popular venue for railway photographers, where the 'Black Fives' and '8Fs' of Rose Grove shed epitomised the dying years of steam — as exampled by '8F' No 48775 working from Todmorden to Burnley with a loaded coal train. With steam gone the line over Copy Pit became something of a back water after the summer of 1968, even though it still carried a considerable number of freight trains and several summer special and excursion workings.
Dave Thomas

Left:
In 1970 the line from Burnley to Todmorden was resignalled, and the section up to Hall Royd Junction was brought under Preston Power Box. Though this development should have ensured a brighter future for the line, BR took to rerouteing trains on other lines and on some days no trains used the route at all — Copy Pit looked a prime candidate for closure, but it survived. On 16 August 1989 No 56097 heads west through Portsmouth with 6E80 the 10.30am Deepdale (Preston)-Healey Mills Speedlink coal empties.
Paul D. Shannon

tion, from where the branch line up to Stainland diverged. Though passenger services on this branch ceased in 1929, the station remained a useful connection on the main line for Halifax until 1962.

Elland was the first station for Halifax, though it could hardly be considered as being convenient. A horse-bus operated up into the town, whilst the local carters enjoyed a lucrative trade trans-shipping goods until the Halifax branch opened four years later. The first station was constructed from timber and located close against the eastern entrance to Elland Tunnel, but this was resited in 1865 when a stone building was erected at the eastern end of the original platforms. A third and final station was provided at a cost of almost £11,000 in connection with the line improvements of the late-Victorian period and came into service in February 1894. Its island platforms remained an important facility in the area, but the loss of the goods (June) and passenger (September) services in 1962 were a cruel blow for a town of this size.

The passenger service to Brighouse was to last a little longer, finally being withdrawn in January 1970. This was a particularly tragic decision, for the well-patronised station had been the first railhead for Bradford. Despite the fact that the connecting stage-coach journey took 1½ hours alone, an average of 8,000 people a week used it. Brighouse declined somewhat after the opening of the Mirfield-Low Moor line, but it still generated a substantial level of local traffic. A direct line from Brighouse to Bradford had been desired for many years, not only as a short cut, but as a means to serve the industrial area around Bailiff Bridge. This goal was achieved in March 1881 when the 'Pickle Bridge' branch opened, providing a west-facing junction at Wyke and an east-facing one at Anchor Pit on the main line, a little to the east of Brighouse. The scheme had first been envisaged back in the late 1840s, but had been abandoned a few years later only to be reintroduced several times before work began in 1874. Intermediate stations were provided at Clifton Road (for Brighouse) and Bailiff Bridge, on a line which was heavily engineered.

With the growth in rail traffic experienced in the late 19th century, the old M&L was becoming exceptionally overcrowded, and the L&YR decided that the line would have to be quadrupled. Contracts were let around the turn of the century, as pressure was growing due to traffic coming off the Huddersfield-Manchester (Standedge) line at Heaton Lodge. This new work was to cost £137,000 for the section down to Horbury, and involved the construction of a new station at Brighouse in 1893.

The final line to discuss in this section is the short cut-off route from Bradley Wood to Bradley station, which was opened by the LNWR to allow a connection from Huddersfield to Manchester. However after the opening of the Standedge route it was largely unnecessary, and it fell into disuse before being sold to the L&YR. For them it was an ideal short cut to get into Huddersfield and they carried out several improvements, though the expenditure was not really justified until after the opening of the 'Pickle Bridge' branch. Its last regular passenger use was a summer Saturday Bradford-Weymouth service which vanished in the early 1980s, after which it became largely a freight only line with the occasional excursion train. Today it is disused, but is retained in anticipation of the Huddersfield-Halifax service, which it is hoped will be introduced by the West Yorkshire PTE in the 1993-94 financial year.

Cooper Bridge

Cooper Bridge station was originally built on the west side of the road which is now the A62, its principal task being to serve the distant town of Huddersfield. It was never a very busy station after the opening of the Huddersfield & Manchester Railway, yet, in preparation for the quadrupling of the line, a new island station was built on the opposite side of the road. It continued in use until 1950 after which the ornate entrance from the road was blocked up, though goods traffic lasted up to September 1963.

Beyond Cooper Bridge came Heaton Lodge, where the H&MR trailed in from the west. When the direct route opened through to Manchester in 1849, this became an exceptionally busy junction but it experienced even more traffic following the opening of the LNWR's 'New Line' to Leeds in 1900. The convergence of two trans-Pennine routes and the start of a Midland Railway branch on the shared section of track between Heaton Lodge and Thornhill junctions made signalling exceptionally difficult until the LMS introduced its speed signalling system in the 1930s. The new system was based on an American practice using coloured light signals to indicate to drivers the speeds and routes to be taken. It lasted until July 1963, when a new system of colour-light signals was introduced in conjunction with the new power signal box at Healey Mills. In more recent times the reduction to double track of both trans-Pennine lines has led to a major simplification of the junction, though the eastbound 'New Line' underpass tunnels below the M&L has been retained to prevent conflicting movements between fast express services and freight workings.

Mirfield

Next came the site of Mirfield MPD which, until closure in 1967, was another of the important freight-loco sheds alongside the main line. Where the line crosses the River Calder at Mirfield, a two-track bridge caused considerable congestion after the rest of the line had been quadrupled. This problem was resolved in the 1930s when the LMS erected a new iron bridge alongside the original stone structure. Mirfield passenger station was originally constructed with two platforms straddling the running lines, but the facilities were so poor that the local paper commented that 'The Lancashire & Yorkshire Railway Company, thought of erecting nothing more than a small wood shed — a kind of box — for the convenience of passengers at Mirfield'. In 1845 a more substantial station was constructed but the growing number of trains soon outgrew the facilities, particularly after the partial opening of the Mirfield-Bradford route. When that line was completed in May 1850, Mirfield took on the role of an important junction station and became the main station for Bradford-Manchester traffic, but conditions were still very poor.

The foundation stone of the third station was laid on 18 March 1865, and work was quickly completed at a cost £17,500. Even so the connections offered for the Bradford branch were still very poor and the L&YR decided to provide a hotel, buffet and bil-

Facing page, top:
By the mid-1960s the decline in the railways was becoming particularly marked. With evidence of rationalisation all too clear, a rake of Class 110 DMUs heads east towards Sowerby Bridge station on 29 May 1967.
C. T. Gifford

Facing page, bottom:
A decade later, on 4 April 1978, the scene has changed subtly. The water tower on the north side of the line has been converted to part of a new warehouse and the number of arms on the semaphore gantry has been reduced. None the less, Sowerby Bridge West box remains — and looks to be in good condition — and, in the distance, can be seen the attractive station buildings. Also visible, to the east of the station, is the warehouse built on the trackbed of the now-closed Ripponden branch.
G. W. Morrison

Above left:
The new order on the Calder Valley line: Class 158 No 158810 departs from Sowerby Bridge with the 12.48 York-Liverpool via Bradford and Halifax service on 18 June 1992. Although the town scape has stayed remarkably unchanged since 1978, the railway has continued to see its facilities reduced. Gone are the remaining sidings, the signal gantry and the attractive signalbox whilst substantial bushes have grown up to shield the railway from the buildings constructed around the site of the former water tower. *Gavin Morrison*

liards room for passengers' comfort — overlooking the obvious solution, improving the connections! To the east of the station were extensive sidings in the midst of which was Cleckheaton Junction, where the Bradford line diverged. A little further on, at Ravensthorpe, the Leeds, Dewsbury & Manchester Railway diverged starting the direct route to Leeds via Dewsbury and Morley — a route which L&YR trains began using shortly after it opened in 1848.

Today the LD&M route carries the main trans-Pennine passenger services, which then use the M&L line to Heaton Lodge, before turning off to Huddersfield on the H&M. Mirfield is therefore the only station still in regular use between Sowerby Bridge and Wakefield. The original overall roof was demolished in the 1970s, the lengthy platforms have since been cut back and the buildings removed. A third platform came into use in 1990, situated on the slow/local line and used by stopping trains to Huddersfield. This basic timber-built affair is situated on the opposite side of the underline road bridge, thus making the station a far cry from the L&YR's concept of convenience.

Thornhill & Dewsbury

Dewsbury's first rail connections came at Thornhill, with the opening of the Calder Valley line and it remained as the town's only station until the LD&M opened. Even then Thornhill station was still called Dewsbury until 1851, despite the fact it was some distance south of the town itself. In 1846, the M&L proposed a branch into the centre of Dewsbury, but the powers granted by Parliament were allowed to lapse. Consequently Thornhill grew in importance, becoming a station with extensive passenger, goods and trans-ship facilities.

Access into the centre of Dewsbury was provided by the L&YR when a branch was opened to the Market Place, from which the new station took its name. The line opened to goods traffic in August 1866, with passenger trains commencing the following April. The branch began at a triangular junction east of Thornhill, in the centre of which the L&YR opened its Thornhill Carriage Works in 1878. Provision of a large goods yard at Dewsbury Market Place somewhat reduced the volume of traffic at Thornhill station, but both continued to be fully used during the textile boom of the 1870s. In 1887 an inter-company spur was opened at Headfield, to connect the L&YR and GNR lines by a girder bridge spanning the river. It was intended for goods exchange, but very soon the benefit of co-operation in passenger traffic was noticed. From 1893 the spur was used to facilitate a vital connection in a circular L&YR/GNR Leeds-Batley-Cleckheaton-Dewsbury-Batley-Leeds passenger service.

When rationalisation was instituted after the Grouping, Dewsbury Market Place became one of the first major casualties, for in 1930 passenger traffic ceased, and three years later the last scheduled train ran over the Headfield spur and it fell into disuse. Thornhill did somewhat better and passenger trains lasted until 1954. Though Market Place remained open to goods traffic, it was only one of four large yards serving the town centre. Goods traffic from Market Place ceased in February 1961 and Thornhill station closed completely the following January. But in order to allow access to the GNR yard the Headfield spur was reinstated, and once again goods trains began running over Dewsbury East Junction in 1965. However, this yard has closed in recent years and the short stub of the branch trailing from the East Junction now only serves the Blue Circle cement terminal on the site of the old carriage works.

Healey Mills & Horbury

Shortly after Dewsbury, the valley of the River Calder begins to widen as the line progresses towards Wakefield. This was always a very busy section, for after Dewsbury East Junction there followed a succession of other junctions as lines diverged towards South Yorkshire. These commenced with the Midland Junction at Thornhill where the West Riding Extension of the Midland Railway from Royston to Dewsbury threw off a spur to the L&YR main line. Beyond here was the small goods yard at Healey Mills, situated just before Horbury & Ossett Station. Immediately after that station came the junction for the Barnsley branch, which opened on 1 January 1850 and merged into the L&YR exactly eight years later. Where the eastern arm of the branch line's triangular junction joined the main line came Horbury Junction Station, which also opened in 1850 having been constructed in connection with the Barnsley branch.

On the approach to Kirkgate the M&L was crossed by the Leeds-Doncaster line, which was carried above it at right-angles by a brick viaduct. On the far side of this a sharply curved line trailed back from Ings Road and climbed up the steep gradient to Westgate. When the Horbury-Wakefield section of the

Below right:
The West Riding town of Greetland was an important junction, with lines heading both north towards Halifax and south towards the branch terminus at Stainland & Holywell Green. Looking westwards along the station towards the junction with the Halifax branch, the photographer has caught both up and down platform buildings, as well as the junction itself. On the eastbound platform is one of a number of replacement signalboxes constructed by the LMS in the late 1930s onwards built to an ARP specification to minimise bomb damage in the event of war.
Real Photos/Ian Allan Library

Bottom right:
The branch service to Stainland was an early victim, closing in 1929 although freight was to survive for a further 30 years, and Greetland itself lost its passenger services on 12 September 1962. With the withdrawal of the (Manchester-)Sowerby Bridge-York direct service over the Calder Valley main line in January 1970 the only passenger trains to pass through the now-demolished station were rare services running from Halifax towards Huddersfield. These, too, have now ceased and the Greetland Junction-Dryclough Junction line is currently mothballed. If current plans come to fruition, however, a new service with reopened stations will link Halifax with Huddersfield. In amongst the decimation of the railway network, the 'switched out' Greetland box remains a fixture on 16 March 1992.
Author

main line was quadrupled, it involved extensive construction work which included the filling in of a low viaduct outside Wakefield and the opening out of the 128yd-long Horbury Tunnel. The new four-track line necessitated the remodelling of Horbury Junction, the closure of the junction station (on 11 July 1927) and the opening of a new station at Millfield Road on the main line in between the east and west junctions.

In 1963 British Railways opened a major hump marshalling yard for the Wakefield District on 140 acre site on farmland based around the old L&YR sidings at Healey Mills. This scheme cost £3¾ million and was orchestrated under the British Transport Commission's 1957 modernisation programme, being envisaged as *the* means to revolutionise goods traffic in the district — particularly coal. Freight patterns had altered greatly during the postwar years, as rail-borne traffic shrank in the face of fierce road competition. Consequently, BR began rationalising handling capacity, and locally 13 goods yards were closed as they moved away from the part-load business. On 23 July the new yard opened, complete with flood-lighting to allow 24-hour operation. A few private delivery sidings were left to serve the rest of the area, but most of these were earmarked for closure within a 10-year period. It was also provided with a diesel locomotive depot, permitting the gradual closure of the ex-L&YR sheds at Low Moor, Mirfield, Sowerby Bridge and Wakefield. Meanwhile the two stations at Horbury have long since passed into oblivion; Millfield Road being removed in 1961 and Horbury & Ossett closing after the withdrawal of the York-Sowerby Bridge service in January 1970.

Wakefield

The first station to serve Wakefield was at Oakenshaw, on the North Midland Railway line which opened in July 1840 linking Rotherham with Leeds. Though this station originally bore the name Wakefield, just a few

Below left:
The last surviving member of the Hughes Class 4-6-0s, No 56455, works its final excursion through Brighouse in 1951. Though not a standard LMS class, several of these powerful engines lasted into BR days and still had plenty of life in them when they were withdrawn. Around this time my father regularly used this line to travel between his firm's offices in Brighouse and Elland but, as a consequence of Elland's closure in 1962, our first car (an Austin A35) was purchased and like many other families of that era we turned our back on the railways!
The late Frank Alcock

Bottom left:
The remains of Brighouse station today, seen on 21 June 1992, are but a sad reminder of the decline of the railways over the past 30 years. Although the platforms survive, albeit heavily overgrown, few passengers will have made use of them since the withdrawal of regular passenger services from Sowerby Bridge along the Calder Valley to Wakefield on 5 January 1970. It could be, however, that Brighouse will have a future as a passenger station; West Yorkshire PTE are actively pursuing the reopening of the line from Halifax to Huddersfield through Brighouse, with the possibility of new stations at Brighouse and Elland.
Gavin Morrison

Above:
Another stretch of the former L&YR network to be currently mothballed is that from Bradley Wood Junction to Bradley Junction. Again, if the plan to restore a passenger service to the Halifax-Huddersfield route comes to fruition this link will be restored.
Author

Below right:
Cooper Bridge holds an interesting place in railway history, for it was here that the first railway ticket issuing equipment was tried out. The system was devised by Thomas Edmondson whilst he was working on the Newcastle & Carlisle Railway, but that company were not interested in his ideas to prevent ticket fraud. Accordingly he approached the M&L, and in turn they offered him facilities to experiment at Cooper Bridge, where the system proved to be an immediate success, catching several fraudsters in the first few months. After further refinements it eventually became the standard railway ticket in Britain, and was widely used elsewhere. Sadly the system was not suitable for today's computerised booking systems, and in more recent years the old $2\frac{9}{32}$in x $1\frac{7}{32}$in pasteboard cards have been phased out and replaced with credit-card sized tickets.
Huddersfield Examiner

months later a more convenient station was built at Kirkgate on the Manchester & Leeds line. The construction of the M&L had taken some considerable time, and though the terrain around Wakefield was not as difficult as the Pennine countryside, it had not been an easy task. Considerable opposition had been demonstrated by the Aire & Calder Navigation Co, and the matter resulted in extensive litigation before the railway could be built. Past Wakefield the Calder had to be completely diverted at Kirkthorpe to avoid the costly expense of two large bridges, and the ox-bow lake to the south of the line still bears testimony to that diversion.

When the M&L opened throughout in 1841 the NM station was renamed Oakenshaw, but the facilities at Kirkgate were far from adequate as the buildings were very basic. The difficulties of station accommodation were considerably increased when the WP&GR route to Goole opened in 1848. As the Askern branch of this line made an end-on junction with the GNR, this created an additional traffic flow from that system, which worsened the serious congestion at Wakefield. In 1849 an interesting connection was provided with the Smithson Tramway, which ran from Low Laithes to Thornes Wharf on the River Calder, involving a hoist at the west end of the station which lowered wagons down to the tramway. By 1853 a solution to the problem of overcrowding at Wakefield was found when the L&YR agreed to build a joint station with the GNR, and then appoint a joint committee for its management. The completed station came into use in 1857, and basically comprised a long main platform and a new island, with the whole being covered by an overall roof.

A major development of the area's rail network had come with the Bradford, Wakefield & Leeds Railway which converted a private house into a station at Westgate. The spur from the BW&L line to Ings Road Junction, allowed the L&YR to run into the new station and also led to the introduction of a through GNR service to Leeds via both of Wakefield's stations. With the promotion of the West Riding & Grimsby Joint Railway in 1864, a new station was designed allowing the closure of the first Westgate station on 1 May 1867. One of the most significant 'freight'

Left:
A westbound 'right away' goods waits a clear signal before restarting from Heaton Lodge, behind 'A' class 0-6-0 No 1243. However, the picture reveals far more information as careful observation of the scene will show. In the immediate foreground are the rough colliery tracks of the Battye Bank 'day hole' (or drift mine), whilst on the opposite side of the fence the fogman's hut is to be seen. To the rear a pair of lines running towards a girder bridge over the River Calder are in fact the LNWR's 'New Line' to Leeds, possibly still incomplete at this time.
Bucknall Collection/Ian Allan Library

Left:
Mirfield station is reputed to be the very first of its kind, being designed as an 'island' with two main platform faces and bays at either end and covered by an overall roof. This concept provided direct access to every single platform, without passengers having to resort to crossing running lines. Whether it really was the first of its type is open to debate, but on its opening in 1866 railway engineers from all over the world came to examine its design. Sadly the train shed was removed in the mid-1970s and the platforms have been repeatedly cut back. A third platform has now been erected on the local line and the ensuing facility is really rather poor. On 17 June 1990 No 47519 on a Liverpool-Newcastle service passes DMU No 144018 on a Leeds-Marsden train.
John Bateman

lines in the area was the cut-off route from Kirkgate to the GNR at Hare Park which, in addition to its intended purpose, formed a useful operating link that allowed GNR/LNER trains to use Kirkgate station when Westgate was blocked. A long standing bottleneck, the two-track west-end approach to Kirkgate, was resolved by the quadrupling programme instituted by the L&YR at the start of the present century. Work in the Wakefield area commenced in 1901 and was completed by the LMS in 1927-28.

The postwar rationalisation after the formation of British Railways led to a gradual withdrawal of local services, and the ex-GNR lines were badly affected by closures in the early 1950s. In April 1960 BR introduced a new Leeds-Sheffield DMU service which ran via Wakefield Kirkgate and the Barnsley branch, but the withdrawal of other local services continued apace throughout the next five years. A new concourse was erected at Westgate station in 1967, but during the same year the service to Pontefract was withdrawn. Thereafter the bulk of BR's rail development centred on Westgate, with Kirkgate becoming very much the poor relation. For

years this meant that Kirkgate was limited to a basic hourly service between Leeds and Sheffield and one of the same frequency on the route from Huddersfield to Wakefield Westgate. Any idea of using Kirkgate as an interchange was fraught with problems — as the connections between the two services were pretty abysmal, though a planned refurbishment and the introduction of a new service to Pontefract may help the station's fortunes revive to a small extent.

To the east of the station was a large triangular junction where the WP&GR line diverged, in the centre of which was erected the city's first engine shed and which later gave way to a huge carriage shed on the site. Turners Lane Junction marked the end of the complex, and there were no intermediate stations between Wakefield and Goose Hill Junction, where the connections were made with the North Midland (later Midland) line. In 1871 Normanton station was improved when the two small island platforms were demolished and replaced by a single island platform which was nearly a ¼ mile long. In 1884 the Midland built one of their standard engine sheds for use by the L&YR, but the

Above:

Mirfield shed was one of the most important L&YR freight engine sheds east of the Pennines. Pictured in the 1930s, a wide range of locomotives is visible. The variety includes an ex-LNWR 0-8-0, and ex-L&YR 2-4-2T No 10712 (ex-L&YR No 1263) and Fowler 2-6-4T No 2405.
The late Frank Alcock

Centre right:

More than half a century on Mirfield shed still stands, albeit in an increasingly derelict condition and no longer used for its original purpose. Like so many sheds, the decline in the railways and the move to diesel power meant death for many sheds like Mirfield. Other notable L&YR sheds, such as Low Moor, now survive only as memories or in photographs.
Author

Right:

Dewsbury East Junction, with No 42079 drawing a three-coach Wakefield-Low Moor ECS train on 27 July 1948. The newly nationalised locomotive, having been outshopped from Crewe after a major overhaul, was still being run on non-revenue-earning duties by Wakefield shed, and with some justification as it was later returned to the BR works at Horwich for further attention.
The late Frank Alcock

coaling stage was very much to a 'Lanky' pattern.

Normanton became known as the 'Crewe of the Coalfields', and was one of the largest junction stations in the area, but it has suffered terribly since the coal industry went into decline. The facilities today are just a shadow of the once-magnificent station, and Normanton is little more than a halt for DMUs on the service from Sheffield to Leeds via Barnsley — everything else has finished.

Decline and Decay

The 1950s and early 1960s were a bad time for the old M&L line, despite the introduction of new DMU sets specially designed for the route. Thirty three-car sets were ordered, 20 of which were allocated to the North Eastern Region with the remaining ones going to the London Midland Region. The end motor vehicles each had two x 720hp engines, higher than the 600hp rating of normal DMUs. The Calder Valley (TOPS Class 110) sets could make light work of the steeply graded lines, and this was clearly demonstrated when the LMR had to substitute Craven DMUs when one of their 10 sets was out of service. Even so, the basic problem was the loss of the area's traditional traffic flows, a symptom specifically generated by the decline in the textile and coal-mining industries. Not only did this affect freight, but as towns adjacent to the route suffered from a localised depression, passenger numbers also began to drop. This was compounded as long-established industries closed down and the region struggled to readjust, so rail travel became something of a luxury.

At the same time the railways were having to face stiff competition from bus operators, with their cheaper fares, whilst private car ownership was also increasing. All of which was coincidental with a continuing increase in rail fares as losses rose and the level of subsidies declined. In turn these conditions led to even lower numbers travelling by rail, which

Below left:
There have been several proposals for reopening a station at Thornhill to serve south Dewsbury, but so far nothing has materialised and passengers have had to make do with the ex-LNWR station on the Leeds, Dewsbury & Manchester line. Though this line was a competitor of the L&YR it was closely associated with the 'Lanky' and depended on it for access to the Huddersfield & Manchester Railway, at Heaton Lodge. In fact, after the LD&M opened in 1849, the L&YR took to rerouteing several express workings over that route thus shortening the journey time to Leeds. In January 1991, a newly introduced Class 158 (No 158739) is piloted off the LD&M and over Thornhill Junction on to the M&L main line following a fire which destroyed the Down platform buildings.
Author

Bottom left:
Throughout the late 19th century, the approach to Wakefield caused continual problems due to the two track layout. The slow coal trains that were predominant on this section moved from block section to block section, an interminably slow process for the crews and frustrating for passengers on express trains which frequently got held up as a result. Accordingly the L&YR decided to improve the situation by quadrupling, and this work proceeded in stages, the last of which was from Mirfield to Wakefield. Some work was carried out early in the 20th century, but it fell to the LMS to complete the most difficult stage on the approach to Wakefield. Shortly after the Grouping, but still carrying L&YR plates, 0-8-0 No 411 passes through Horbury on a loaded coal train in 1923.
Real Photographs/Ian Allan Library

43

was instrumental in a further withdrawal of services. Then, in January 1970, the line lost its scheduled express passenger services as all trans-Pennine trains were concentrated on the Huddersfield route. This had a pronounced effect on local services, and on the east side of the Pennines the section between Heaton Lodge and Milner Royd has been devoid of regular passenger services for the last two decades.

During the last few years a slight improvement has been noted, at least as far as most of the route is concerned. The reintroduction of frequent trains to Blackpool and the new half-hourly Class 158 Calder Valley trans-Pennine service has done much to improve the section from west of Sowerby Bridge. Regretfully none of these trains use the main line below Milner Royd, though they do provide a useful 15min frequency service between Leeds/Bradford and Halifax. The advent of this intensive frequency has presented difficulties with regard to providing the proposed stations at Low Moor and Salterhebble, as stops at these points would considerably affect the current schedule. However, if a few of the Class 158 workings could be rerouted via Wakefield and Brighouse it would surely fill a much needed gap in the local rail network. Likewise one wonders why trains from Manchester to Burnley could not be run via Todmorden, as this could be considerably quicker than the present circuitous route via Bolton and Blackburn. Though the Calder Valley line remains intact, most of the four-track sections have reverted to double track only. Generally speaking, the services are better than they have been for many years, but one wonders what George Stephenson, Barnard Dickinson or John Aspinall would think if they could see the line today!

Right:
History has shown the great marshalling yards that were being completed in the early 1960s to be little more than 'White Elephants', and it is interesting to note that at the time of their conception many railwaymen seriously doubted the wisdom of the scheme. To them and enthusiasts alike, it was clear to see that traffic patterns were already changing towards block trains and the need for frequent marshalling was rapidly disappearing. Healey Mills is a product of that era and, though some trains still call there for crew changing, the yard is now closed. On 21 August 1988, No 37308 departs with the daily Speedlink coal train to Scotland, including Russell containers and HEA hoppers.
Paul D. Shannon

Right:
To conclude the section on the L&YR main line, we will look at its gradual decline which began in the 1960s and accelerated through the 1970s and 1980s. As local services on the M&L went over to DMU operation, steam retained its entrenched stronghold on freight and the express workings. However, it was very much a rearguard action that was being fought as '8F' 2-8-0 No 48276 drifts over Cornholme Viaduct on a Bradford-Blackpool relief on 4 August 1962.
T. S. Greenwood

The **1960s** shift from rail to
road was something of a
national trend, but instead of
improving services and
lowering fares, the
Government's solution was
the appointment of Dr
Beeching to form a report on
*The Re-shaping of British
Railways*. This had a
pronounced effect on the
industrial north, and the
Calder services were greatly
pruned. Modernisation
stemmed the flow, and by
1962 most steam-hauled
passenger working over the
Calder Valley route had been
largely replaced by DMU
operations. Even so, stations
like Wakefield Kirkgate
continued to witness loco-
hauled passenger trains as in
1965 when Brush Type **4**
No D1511 passed through
with a diverted working for
King's Cross.
The late Eric Treacy

Normanton was a very
important joint station,
shared by the North Midland
Railway, M&L and the York
& North Midland Railway
(later NER), though managed
solely by the NMR. There
was also an important hotel
facility which was connected
to the station by a footbridge
to allow passengers to break
their journey for a meal in
the days before on-train
catering. A Channel Tunnel
freight terminal planned for
Normanton has recently been
overturned after bitter
opposition by local residents,
and the outcome has now
seen a proposal to shift the
terminal to a site near
Whitwood. However, an ash-
disposal plant has been
recently opened near the site
of Goose Hill Junction, and
on 25 October **1991** No **56088**
draws a train-load of shale
from Selby through the new
facility.
Paul D. Shannon

3

Merseyside & West Lancashire

The Liverpool & Bury Railway

Though the L&B was the L&YR's principal line into Liverpool, its development is more correctly associated with Greater Manchester and it is therefore described in Chapter 6. However, it is appropriate to commence this chapter with a short description of the line which was authorised in July 1845, and was projected from a site near the Borough Gaol in Liverpool to the MB&RR at Bury, along with a short branch from Upholland to Skelmersdale. Work began early in 1846, and involved some considerable feats of engineering, the most significant being Liverpool viaduct which was over one mile long and had 117 arches. Then there was a 1,149yd-long tunnel through a sandstone ridge at Walton; this tunnel was an easy one to drive, but the 959yd bore at Upholland was both difficult and wet. Lord Derby's Moss was another major obstacle, and a variety of methods had to be employed before a stable foundation could be obtained.

The line opened to through traffic in November 1848, but work on the L&B branch to Skelmersdale had already been suspended in 1848, and some 10 years were to elapse before it finally reached completion. By this time the L&YR and ELR had merged, and it was a through line from Rainford to Ormskirk that eventually opened on 1 March 1858 — at the same time a new station at Rainford Junction replaced the earlier one at Rainford.

As mentioned elsewhere in this book, the L&B became the alternative route from Manchester to Liverpool and, once the Atherton and Pemberton lines had opened, the new L&YR 'direct' route enjoyed a substantial level of patronage. This continued down through the LMS era, but under BR the benefits of a second main line to Liverpool were not really valued and the slow process of closure by stealth began. The Atherton line has faced repeated threats over the years, but it still remains extant. From Liverpool the EMUs run out from Moorfields, rejoining the original L&YR line not far from the site of the old Exchange station. They then travel north to the staffed station at Sandhills, passing through the site of the projected station for Vauxhall. At Sandhills Junction the line parts company with the route to Southport, and then immediately encounters the Kirk-

dale EMU depot which is located in the 'V' of the junction. Though the depot occupies a large site, it is nothing compared to the former Sandhills (Bank Hall) shed which once possessed two separate eight-road sheds.

Kirkdale station is now very basic, and sits forlornly in a large excavated area once full of carriage sidings. However, most of the tracks have now been lifted and only one bore of the twin tunnels remains in use, but the old 'Kirkdale Cutting' sign is still *in situ*. Beyond the tunnels, the LO&P line diverges at Walton Junction. However, the station at Preston Road has been replaced by more basic facilities at Rice Lane. The line used to pass below the Midland and CLC lines, but only the abutments of these high over-line bridges now remain. Fazakerley is the penultimate stop for the Class 507s and shortly the track becomes single for the final stint to Kirkby where the electric service now terminates, it was once intended to electrify the entire route with a third-rail system as far as Wigan but this has never materialised.

Liverpool, Ormskirk & Preston Railway

In the summer of 1844 a scheme emerged for a railway linking Liverpool and Preston via Ormskirk, from which point a branch would diverge to Southport. However, this promotion was violently opposed by the Liverpool & Manchester and North Union railways, as it would shorten the existing route to Preston by nine and three-quarter miles. Similarly the Southport proposal incurred the wrath of the M&L and LC&S railways. Yet despite this opposition, the Bill was approved on 16 August 1846. The Southport branch was not approved, but two others (from Kirkdale to Liverpool Docks and from Ormskirk to Skelmersdale) were. Meanwhile, in July 1845 the LO&P was amalgamated into the East Lancashire Railway and from October 1846 its activities were controlled from the company's offices in Bury.

Work commenced in March 1847, but difficult crossings over large tracts of low-lying marshy ground created immense difficulties, particularly at Rufford. Yet, within exactly two years of the work commencing, it reached completion, and trains began running in April 1849. The LO&P left the L&B at Walton on the Hill, and ended where it joined the NUR at Penwortham near Pres-

Above:
Between Liverpool (Great Howard Street) and Orrell there were intermediate stations at Bootle Lane (later Sandhills), Preston Road, Simonswood (which became Aintree L&YR and later Fazakerley), Kirkby, Rainford, Pimbo Lane and Upholland. Between the original stations at Orrell and Upholland there was a distance of just 1¾ miles, which was something of an over provision. Accordingly Upholland closed in 1852 when Orrell became Orrell & Upholland, but in 1900 it reverted to its original title when Pimbo Lane became the third Upholland station. Fazakerley is still extant, but considerably less attractive than in this rural view at the turn of the century.
B. C. Lane Collection

Left:
The modernised station at Fazakerley remains open, served by the third-rail EMUs on the Liverpool-Kirkby route. The platform level buildings have been replaced and a new booking hall is located at road level. Two Class 507s, Nos 507013 and 507016, pass at the station in March 1992. *Author*

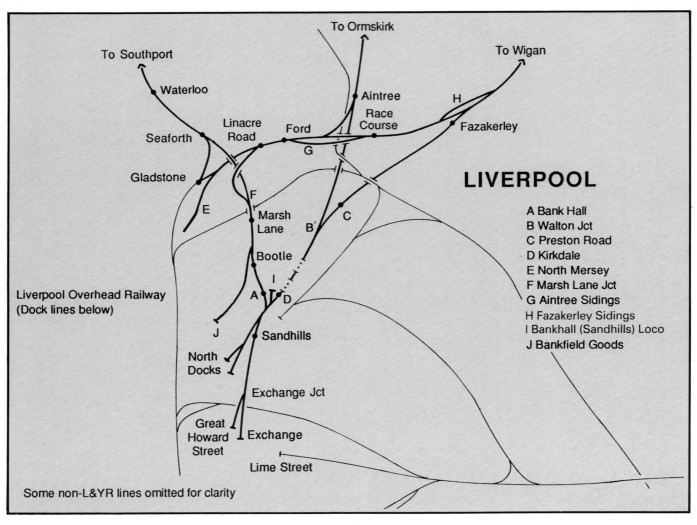

To Southport

Waterloo

To Ormskirk

To Wigan

Aintree
Race
Course

Seaforth

Linacre
Road

Ford

H

Fazakerley

Gladstone

E

F

Marsh
Lane

B

G

C

LIVERPOOL

A Bank Hall
B Walton Jct
C Preston Road
D Kirkdale
E North Mersey
F Marsh Lane Jct
G Aintree Sidings
H Fazakerley Sidings
I Bankhall (Sandhills) Loco
J Bankfield Goods

Bootle

I

Liverpool Overhead Railway
(Dock lines below)

A

D

J

Sandhills

North
Docks

Exchange Jct

Great
Howard
Street

Exchange

Lime Street

Some non-L&YR lines omitted for clarity

ton. A further connection at Farrington permitted the LO&P to make an end on junction with the ELR. Intermediate stations on the line were at Walton Junction, Aintree, Maghull, Town Green & Aughton, Ormskirk, Burscough, Rufford, Croston, and Lostock Hall. A further station was built at Cocker Hall in 1851 but this closed in 1859 and was replaced by Midge Hall three-quarters of a mile nearer Preston. In the years which followed later additions were Aughton Park, Old Roan and Orrell Park.

The development of the route between Liverpool and Preston was one of steady if not spectacular progress, which was aided by the joint ELR/L&YR line from Burscough to Southport. The principal traffic flow was to/from the mill towns of north Lancashire, with 'King Cotton' providing the all-important base on which such traffic developed. Passenger trains to Preston suffered from the disadvantage of an annoying reversal at Lostock Hall, but this was eventually resolved by the construction of a series of curves near Farrington. Once the ELR and L&YR had merged in 1859, the company enjoyed a virtual monopoly of the whole of the area to the north of Liverpool, and the services reflected

this. In 1906 the Skelmersdale branch went over to rail-motor operation, encouraging the provision of new halts at Westhead, White Moss and Heys. During the same year the line from Marsh Junction to Aintree (opened to goods in 1866), saw the introduction of an electric passenger service to Liverpool via Bootle. The line to Ormskirk was also to benefit from the progress of electric traction, and the Liverpool-Aintree section (via Kirkdale) was also electrified in 1906. The service was extended to Maghull in 1909, Town Green in 1911, and eventually to Ormskirk in 1913. As part of the electrification, overhead wires were installed at the Aintree sorting sidings in 1911.

The LMS slightly rationalised services on the through line to Preston, but with the exception of a number of post-World War 2 freight service withdrawals, the line continued pretty much as it had done in L&YR days (locomotive and rolling-stock changes apart). However, passenger trains were withdrawn between Ormskirk and Rainford Junction on Bonfire Night 1956, and the goods services on this section were terminated just five years later! In 1963 the remaining stub of the branch from the Ormskirk end was closed,

Left:
At Kirkby the line of the former Liverpool & Bury Railway is now split, and buffers prevent any progress for through traffic to Manchester. Passengers must therefore get out, walk along the platform and board one of the DMUs which still ply the line through to Wigan and beyond! On 18 August 1991 No 507013 waits quietly for the Bolton train, after arriving with the noon working from Liverpool.
Martin Eltham

Left:
The world-renowned Aintree race meetings, which include the Grand National, involved the L&YR/LMS in a phenomenal level of traffic, but by making use of the sorting sidings or the circular route back into Liverpool, excursion trains were quickly moved out of the station to convenient stabling points. Local trains were all electric-hauled on race days, but the normal sets were replaced by race trains made up of seven six-wheeled coaches with an electric motor-car at each end. Long distance services, such as those from stations in Yorkshire, were loco-hauled trains of up to 16-coaches. In 1928 the engine for one such train, a Hughes 4-6-0 No 10418, awaits its return journey.
Real Photographs/Ian Allan Library

Left:
Aintree L&YR became well known to railwaymen, notably due to the large sorting sidings which opened in 1886. These were the biggest sidings on the system but have long been removed. However, the old eight-road engine shed, which also opened in 1886, still remains, albeit in a very derelict state. Today a link line crosses over to the stub of the CLC line where there is an Excursion platform and a siding for the Metal Box works; from there Class 40 No 40012 heads for Edge Hill conveying an empty van train in July 1983.
Paul D. Shannon

Right:

Exchange was always a very busy station, but there were four days in the year when it was exceptionally so; these being Grand National Day, Whit Monday, 12 July (Orangemen's Day) and August Bank Holiday. The race trains obviously went to Aintree, but on the other three days the destination was usually Southport. However, as the electric line via Crosby was still busy with commuter traffic, these workings usually went via Ormskirk and Burscough. In LMS days excursions to Blackpool and the Lake District became popular from Exchange. At Easter 1912 Aspinall 2-4-2T No 1338 is being turned in readiness for its next stint of duty.
S. G. Joscelyne courtesy B. C. Lane Collection

Below right:

Traffic to the docks (a subject too complex to deal with in this book) was always substantial, particularly in both World Wars. Freight traffic over the L&YR lines into the dock area was phenomenal, and it remained so right up to the mid-1950s when a small but perceptible flow of freight began to leave the railways. Wapping & Salthouse was the first goods depot to go in 1959, then came Great Howard Street which closed in 1963 along with North Docks Low Level Yard. Bankfield (1965), North Docks - High Level (1966) and Sandhills (1974) completed the major closures. On 22 October 1955, ex-L&YR Pug 0-4-0ST No 51253 trundles beneath the overhead railway near St James's station, when most were blissfully unaware of the fate in store for the dock railway system.
P. J. Kelly

Above:

With the electrification programme of 1903-04, the western side of Exchange (platforms Nos 6 to 10) was taken over for the new services and fitted with a third rail. Platforms Nos 4 and 5 were also available to the electrics, but were rarely used for such (if at all). But by the time closure was approved the station had been reduced considerably in size. Shortly before the end a two-car DMU powers out of the remaining platforms with the 12.53pm to Bolton on 18 March 1977 — obscuring the EMU arriving from Southport on the adjacent line.
P. H. Hanson

and lifting began the following year — precisely when Skelmersdale New Town was being built. One can only wonder at the level of traffic that the line might have generated, if only the branch had been left in place for the electric service to continue beyond Ormskirk. Burscough curves were removed in the mid-1960s, and though feasibility studies for their reintroduction have been carried out in recent years, there is no provision for such investment in the current budgets. The service from Preston to Ormskirk is currently subsidised by Lancashire County Council, and despite recent cut-backs and low off-peak use, services have been stabilised at the present level and are reasonably supported.

Today's single line track from Preston to Ormskirk makes quite an attractive journey, mainly passing through flat countryside occupied by small-holdings and market gardens. The station at Midge Hall closed 30 years ago, and trains now only call here to pick up the token from the signal box. Croston is very basic but still open, though Rufford has a very attractive station where a section of double track has been retained for passing purposes. The train then runs southwest alongside the Leeds-Liverpool Canal to Burscough where the LO&P crosses the Wigan-Southport line. At Ormskirk the DMU service from Preston terminates, and like Kirkby the track is split by a pair of buffers and passengers must detrain to progress further south by the EMUs working into Liverpool on the Merseyrail Northern Line.

Beyond Ormskirk the line reverts to double track and then passes through the basic station at Aughton, which is located in a cutting hewn from red sandstone. Town Green seems

quite presentable, whilst a little further to the south a new station is planned to serve Maghull North. Maghull retains its original buildings and canopies on the Liverpool side, but the classic architecture is spoilt by heavy bars on the doors and windows and the present garish blue/cream paint work — posters warning about the penalties of fare-dodging are another 'sign' of the times. A recent provision is the basic timber platform at Old Roan, whilst Aintree station is far removed from the facility prided by the L&YR. The line from Bootle to Fazakerley is now open only as far as Aintree for freight traffic, but there are long term proposals for a passenger service from Liverpool via Bootle. Finally south of Aintree only Orrell Park, with its long platforms, and Walton are encountered before the line joins the former Liverpool & Bury line.

Exchange Station

The terminal point for the L&B in Liverpool was in Great Howard Street, but even before the line opened an extension had been planned into Tithebarn Street. With the LO&PR wishing to make use of the L&B station, when the L&YR commenced work on the extension the cost was jointly shared by the ELR. A substantial amount of engineering work had to be accomplished, and no less than 540 houses, 30 shops, four inns and a chapel had to be demolished to make way for the new station. The two-storey station had an Italianate frontage, which included separate accommodation for both companies and single storey wings containing joint refreshment, waiting and ladies' rooms. It came into use in May 1850, allowing the conversion of

Right:
Discounting Moorfields, which is a modern creation, the last station on the L&YR lines into Liverpool is Sandhills. Its basic platform and bleak appearance are clearly evident in this view of No 507024 on a hazy June morning in 1991. Refurbishment is planned for this station by Merseyrail, but the branch down to the North Docks, pictured to the left of the EMU, has been dismantled to such an extent that it will never carry traffic again, the only access to the once-extensive Mersey Docks & Harbour Board system now being made by a junction from the LC&SR at Bootle.
Martin Eltham

Centre right:
The entire contract for the Southport electrification programme was let to Dick, Kerr & Co Ltd, and the first train ran experimental trials at the end of 1903. The line formally opened for electric traction in March 1904, though the full service did not begin until seven months later when all the four-car sets had been delivered. Initial composition was two first-class and two third-class cars, but on some workings these sets were not sufficient for the numbers of passengers using the trains, and in 1905 several were strengthened by the addition of a fifth car. Conversely some sets were three-car units, as seen in set No 3 working from Southport with a stopping train.
Bucknall Collection/Ian Allan Library

Below right:
When the line was electrified, the L&YR initiated a 10ft wide loading gauge which was the widest in the country up to that time. Today the line maintains an intensified electric service with most trains made up from six-car formations using two x three-car Class 507 EMUs, which are well patronised as evidenced in our photograph. On 5 June 1988 two sets pass at Freshfield, these being the 13.44 train from Liverpool with No 507030 and the 14.00 working out of Southport Chapel Street with No 507012.
Paul D. Shannon

52

Great Howard Street into a goods station with tracks and wagon turntables twisting all over the site and beneath the dark arches of the viaduct.

The traffic using Tithebarn Street (known as Exchange from the 1850s) soon over-taxed the facilities, so the L&YR were forced to make improvements by redesigning the station. One of the major problems was the bottleneck created by the approach roads. This was resolved by the widening of Liverpool viaduct (approved in 1875) which in turn allowed the tracks to be quadrupled. The 'new' station buildings were completed between 1886 and 1888, when a 10-platform terminal came into use and a magnificent 80-bedroom hotel formed part of the complex. Not only did the hotel entertain guests bound for the city of Liverpool, but it was particularly useful for travellers sailing to or from America and beyond.

The station maintained this role throughout the L&YR and LMS era, even after a joint L&YR/LNWR scheme for sharing Manchester traffic had been introduced. However, during the 1960s BR could see little point in duplicate services to the east and Exchange lost most of its principal passenger workings. The station gradually went into decline, with only one half of it being gainfully employed — principally with local workings. After further decline Exchange was closed completely in April 1977 and the electric workings diverted to Moorfields. The former passenger terminus then stood empty, rubbish-strewn and derelict, attracting the attention of vandals until the developers moved in. Today most of the site has been changed out of all recognition, and though the façade of the old station remains, behind it offices have taken the place of railway trains.

Liverpool, Crosby & Southport Railway

Though work on the LC&SR did not commence until March 1848, there had been a proposal for a coastal line from Liverpool to Preston via Southport as early as 1838. While a through route offered considerable promise, at that time there seemed little likelihood of generating much local traffic particularly

Railway Station, Waterloo.

Left:
As the Victorian era progressed, the prosperity which was attached to Liverpool and its docks became reflected in the living standards of the people who worked in the city. It was therefore considered less than desirable to live in the mean back-to-back terrace houses that crowded round the docks and industrial districts, and a slow migration took place to the healthier countryside to the north. Waterloo station, six stops out from Liverpool, was one of the first stations in the commuter belt which stretched northwards along the coast from Seaforth to Southport. It therefore enjoyed an early boom in commuter traffic, which was accentuated greatly after the 1904 electrification.
B. C. Lane

Left:
It is July 1992, almost a century on, and Waterloo station is remarkably unchanged. Although the fifth bay of the awning has disappeared the remaining four still survive despite the loss of their finials.
Gavin Morrison

53

Right:

The value of electric traction continues to be appreciated down to the present day, and a substantial amount of capital equipment has been invested on the Liverpool-Southport service. On 5 May 1983 two EMUs in tandem (Nos 507014/507019) pass Portland Street Box on the outskirts of Southport after leaving Chapel Street with the 18.30 for Liverpool Central.
Paul D. Shannon

Centre right:

When the L&YR acquired the West Lancashire Railway, they were at something of a loss about what to do with it. They eventually decided to close the two WLR terminals and move the services into the joint station at the Preston end and improve Chapel Street in Southport, with a view to moving the line's southern terminus there. The alterations at Southport were achieved in 1901 when the new extension allowed the closure of Central station, which then became Alexandra Road goods depot. Around this time L&YR No 675, one of the 6ft Sharp Stewart 4-4-0s ordered by Barton Wright in 1881, stands in Chapel Street with a train for Blackburn.
Bucknall Collection/Ian Allan Library

Below right:

Class 37/4 No 37415 waits patiently at Southport on 20 March 1992 in Regional Railways livery along with a similarly liveried coach. Although Chapel Street station retains its overall roof, the actual size of the station (as shown in the next pair of illustrations) has been reduced.
Author

north of Southport as most of the communities which the railway would serve were little more than small villages. With the railway north of Southport being dropped (and forming part of a separate proposal), the LC&SR seemed a viable prospect when the single track line opened between Southport and Waterloo in July. Passengers for Liverpool were met at Waterloo by a horse-bus service, until such time as a junction could be made with the joint L&YR/ELR line at Sandhills in October 1850. Southport's single platform terminus at Eastbank Street was a big disadvantage until August the following year, but thereafter an attractively designed station was opened in Chapel Street. The level of traffic soon over-burdened the single line, and it was doubled throughout by September 1852.

The independent LC&SR was a rich prize for the larger railway companies, and though the sale or lease of the line to the M&L had been considered since 1848, the ELR also showed an active interest. By 1854 the L&YR and ELR had almost agreed a joint take-over, but at the last minute a difference arose over terms. The L&YR finally succeeded in gaining sole control in 1855 much to the chagrin of the ELR, a situation which further delayed the merger proposals between those two railways. A further development occurred in 1866 when a cross country line was opened between Bootle and Fazakerley on the Liverpool & Bury line, allowing goods traffic direct access on to the Mersey Docks & Harbour Board system without the need to go into Liverpool. The six mile long line had connections with LO&PR at Aintree and LC&SR at Seaforth, and quickly became a vital link into the northern dock system. In 1880-81 the LNWR opened a branch to Liverpool's Alexandra Dock which passed through a tunnel below the LC&SR near Bootle. Whilst this was primarily intended for freight, it did have an interesting effect on the L&YR line. A joint connection was built between the two lines in 1886, again primarily for goods traffic, but also allowing the commencement of a Southport-Euston service.

By 1903 the traffic between Liverpool and Southport had reached such a magnitude that it was imperative that improvements be made, either by increasing platform lengths and strengthening existing train services or by increasing the frequency of the services. In regard to the first option the costs would be astronomical, whilst the second choice was impossible with conventional steam-hauled services. Accordingly the L&YR decided to adopt electric traction, broadly employing a philosophy that was already in operation on tramways through the length and breadth of Britain. However, the use of such a form of traction had yet to be tried on heavy main line trains. Nevertheless the directors decided to proceed into this new field, and a 7,500V

ac three-phase generating station was erected at Formby — roughly half way between Liverpool and Southport. Sub-stations, where the power supply was stepped down to 620-630V and fed to a third-rail, were erected at strategic locations on the line between Exchange and Crossens. In July 1905 a connection was made with the Liverpool Overhead Railway at Seaforth, allowing the introduction of a Southport-Dingle service using lightweight cars from January 1906 onwards.

Improvements were made to the electric lines by the LMS, beginning in 1927 when new three-car sets were ordered for the Ormskirk/Aintree services. In 1939 sets which had a look of London Underground stock began to enter service, and during the war years the original Newton Heath-built units started to disappear. This was an exceptionally busy line during the period from 1939-45, carrying servicemen to their duties or on leave. Freight traffic also assumed substantial proportions (particularly at night), which was in addition to the normal local traffic to and from Liverpool. The heavy suburban traffic continued into the 1950s, but the Beeching Report saw no future for a commuter service outside London and scheduled the line for closure. His deliberation was based on the fact that Formby power station had closed, and the cost of purchasing the current from the CEGB was too great. If his proposal had been approved it would have been the most ludicrous proposal in a report that contained hundreds of illogical conclusions. Fortunately it was strongly opposed, and after protest letters filled 14 oil drums on the platform at Exchange station the proposal was overruled and the Southport line lives on.

Today the line is well used, and has a frequent service between Liverpool and Southport using Class 507 EMUs. North of Sandhills (due for refurbishment in the near future), the line diverges from the old L&B main line, and immediately runs into the island platform at Bank Hall. Next comes Bootle Junction, where the lines to the docks and Aintree diverge, a short distance before the rather ugly stations at Bootle Oriel Road and Bootle New Strand. For some distance the Aintree line runs parallel with the LC&SR, but this gradually begins to climb up to a flyover by which it crosses the line. Seaforth & Litherland station just has a bus shelter and that is heavily vandalised, meanwhile Waterloo has a more modern set of buildings but these also have a rather squalid appearance. After Blundellsands & Crosby things get a bit better as the line runs on to Hall Road which was once the terminus for the Liverpool suburban trains, a point which is marked by the fact that an EMU depot still stands alongside the line.

North of Hall Road the line opens out into the countryside, where golf courses testify to the existence of suburbia. There then follows

a succession of rural stations — Hightown, Formby, Freshfield, Ainsdale, Hillside and Birkdale — as the line heads on to Southport. Altcar Rifle Range (north of Hightown) closed some 70 years ago, but the rest are clean, presentable and reasonably well kept. Between Hightown and Formby a large red-brick building stands out from the flat countryside to mark the site of the L&YR's innovative generating station. Finally, it should be mentioned that the line still retains its semaphore signals, with very high posts in certain locations, but this is due to change in the not too distant future when an I.E.C.C. signalling system is installed.

Southport & Environs

Though it had been intended to create a railway link to Southport in the first flush of railway-mania, the seaside community was to wait until 1848 when the first line of rails reached the town from Waterloo. During the mid-1840s two other schemes were promoted which would establish links to Preston via Hesketh Bank and Manchester via Wigan.

The first of these proposals quickly vanished, while patience was needed with the Manchester & Southport Railway which seemed in no urgency to build its line beyond Wigan. Meanwhile the LO&PR (ELR) had been defeated in their attempt to build a branch from Ormskirk to Southport. Despite continual pressure from the town's civic leaders, the M&SR (L&YR) showed no inclination to build their line, and, as will be detailed in Chapter Six, were forced into commencing the work only by court action. Beyond Burscough the line was eventually built jointly by the L&YR/ELR and a west-south curve built on to the LO&PR allowed a Liverpool-Ormskirk-Southport service to commence when the line opened in 1855.

Proposals for a direct line to Preston kept re-emerging through the years. However, it was little more than talk until 1870 when Sir T. G. Fermor-Hesketh promoted the Preston & Southport Railway Co. At the first attempt the proposal failed during its Parliamentary passage, only to reappear successfully the following year as the West Lancashire Railway. Construction work began in April 1873, but after a promising start it was halted due to financial difficulties. In 1874 an approach was made to the L&YR to enquire if they would buy or lease the line, but they could see no advantage in so doing. Furthermore, to show they had no need for the direct line the L&YR revived the powers to build a north-west curve at Burscough to allow the introduction of a Southport-Preston service. Even then this curve was not completed until 1878.

The WLR struggled on and after raising further capital resumed work in September 1876, and on 19 February 1878 a 'singularly useless' 7½-mile stretch of railway opened between Hesketh Bank and Hesketh Park. In June the line was extended to a temporary wooden station at Windsor Road, Southport, one mile from Hesketh Park. As if to signify that this railway had no real value, the WLR set about establishing a steam ship fleet in order to provide sailings from Hesketh Bank over the River Ribble to the Fylde Coast, down the Tarleton branch of the Leeds & Liverpool Canal, or further afield to Barrow-in-Furness, Douglas or Port St Mary. The service down the canal apparently brought a substantial level of traffic, though not at any great profit, but even so the directors decided to construct a 1¼-mile long branch from Hesketh Bank to the canal basin at Tarleton. It opened in July 1880, coinciding with the 100th anniversary of the canal branch.

In May 1882 the line was taken three miles nearer to Preston, when a new terminus was opened at Longton. The last stretch into Preston was opened in September 1882, though at that time the station at Fishergate was still not complete. At the same time the new Central station at the Southport end of the line was nearing completion, but even so the sys-

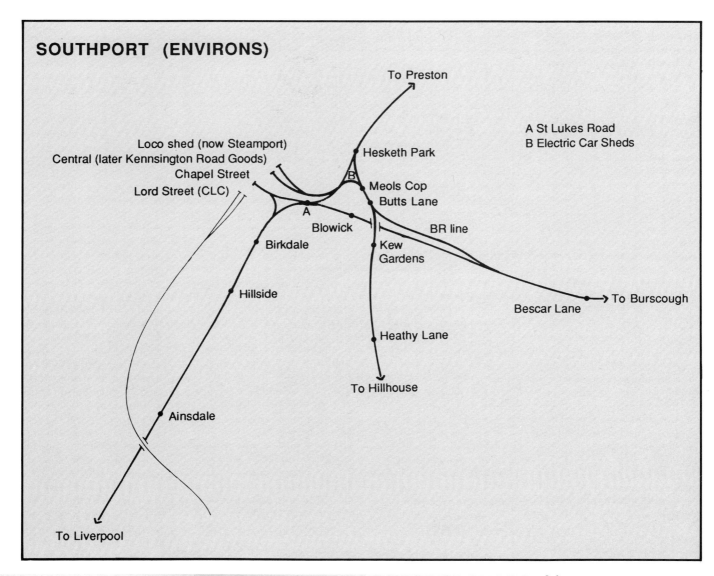

SOUTHPORT (ENVIRONS)

To Preston

A St Lukes Road
B Electric Car Sheds

Loco shed (now Steamport)
Central (later Kennsington Road Goods)
Chapel Street
Lord Street (CLC)

Hesketh Park

Meols Cop
Butts Lane

A

Blowick

BR line

Birkdale

Kew
Gardens

Hillside

Bescar Lane

To Burscough

Heathy Lane

To Hillhouse

Ainsdale

To Liverpool

Left:
The surviving line east from Southport is the former L&YR/ELR line to Burscough Bridge, which is mostly the domain of passenger workings to Manchester via Bolton. It is also used extensively by excursion trains and, to a lesser extent, by freight workings such as this one to the waste disposal terminal at Appley Bridge. On 9 April 1990 No 47440 passes Burscough Bridge Junction cabin. The cabin's name is something of a misnomer now, since the connecting spurs on to the Liverpool, Ormskirk and Preston Railway have been missing for two and a half decades.
Paul D. Shannon

Right:
In 1882 the WLR decided to extend its line to the projected terminus of the Southport & Cheshire Line Extension Railway, but this proposal was defeated and the aimless WLR set about pursuing other schemes to generate traffic for its line. A scheme to link the Hesketh Bank end of the line with Freckleton on the Fylde Coast, by a crossing over the River Ribble, was defeated by Preston Corporation who were anxious to protect the navigable status of the river. The hotch-potch railway was always something of an oddity, not least in its locomotives and rolling stock, a situation reflected in this view of locomotive No 7 *Blackburn*, built in 1862 for the London, Brighton & South Coast Railway. The 2-4-0 had seen 21 years' service around Brighton before being exiled to the muddy coastline of the Ribble Estuary.
Bucknall Collection/Ian Allan Library

Above right:
Southport shed's growing allocation of the late 19th century suggested that substantial extensions would have to be undertaken, but the electrification programme reduced the numbers of 2-4-2 tank engines stabled there from 1904 onwards and it remained a moderately sized shed. Part of the roof was removed by the LMS, and in this portion of the motive power depot ex-L&YR 0-6-0 No 52183 gently simmers in 1950 awaiting its next turn of duty. The shed was closed in June 1965 after substantial withdrawals of locally based steam workings, but it has since become the home of the Steamport railway museum.
Real Photographs/Ian Allan Library

tem was largely isolated from the rest of the railway network. The answer to this problem was seen with links to the LNWR/L&YR joint lines at Preston, and a connection to the Southport & Chester Lines Extension Railway at Hillhouse. The Preston connection opened in 1883 allowing the commencement of a Blackburn-Southport service, but the delays in opening the link to Hillhouse Junction brought about the demise of the WLR which went into receivership in July 1886.

The southern link was to be built by a nominally independent company, the Liverpool, Southport & Preston Junction Railway, but it shared the same offices and officials as the WLR. Though the WLR's failure no doubt affected confidence in the LS&PJR, work went ahead and the seven mile long line opened in September 1887 making a junction with the S&CLER at Downholland at the southern end and a double junction with the WLR at Meols Cop, with through running on to the L&YR system (made possible due to a connection between the S&CLER and the LO&PR at Aintree which had opened in 1880). This development revitalised the WLR, and in 1894 Parliament gave powers

for the company to reconstitute its board of directors and regularise its affairs. The same Act also gave the company a five year 'breathing space' in which no action could be taken against them for debt. However, in 1896 an amalgamation with the L&YR was proposed, and the acquisition went ahead the following July.

In 1904 the Southport electrification scheme took the third-rail system out as far as Crossens on the former WLR section where a good level of commuter traffic originated. Local services on the section from Crossens northwards and on the line from Southport to Hillhouse were lightly used after the electrification of the LC&SR. In 1909 the Hughes railmotors went into service between Southport and Altcar & Hillhouse, with new halts being erected at Butts Lane, Heathey Lane, New Cutt Lane and Plex Moss Lane. The Crossens-Tarleton section was converted in 1912, with a new halt being provided at Boat Yard Crossing, but this was a short lived service which was withdrawn the following year.

In 1911 the Whitehouse curve opened, giving provision for trains from Burscough to run through Meols Cop to St Lukes rather

than running via Blowick. In 1914 further enlargement of Chapel Street was undertaken, involving the demolition of the former ELR station. Excursion traffic remained high throughout the LMS era, but goods traffic down the Tarleton branch was withdrawn in 1930. The LS&PJR section (largely superfluous after the take-over by the L&YR) lost its local passenger trains in September 1938, but remained open for goods traffic and an occasional 'special' until July 1952. Thereafter the line was cut back to Shirldey Hill, and became used for the storage of carriage stock. The WLR was a victim of Beeching, and went at one fell swoop in September 1964, despite the fact that the through trains were still very well used.

Today the routes out of Southport are the LC&SR and the M&S lines, which generate sufficient traffic to keep six platforms at Chapel Street station in service. Numbers one to three are used by the Liverpool-Southport electrics, whilst number four serves trains to Manchester — numbers five and six are largely used for excursion traffic. All the east-bound trains now run out via the Whitehouse Curve, as the section from St Lukes to Pool

Hey junction is closed - the station at St Lukes closed in 1968, though Blowick lost its passenger trains just after the outbreak of World War 2. The island station at Meols Cop still has much of its original character, and is delightfully kept. Bescar Lane is a rather basic station, but what remains has been pleasantly painted in the old L&YR colour scheme. The staggered station at New Lane is an interesting example of railway development, with the original low stone platforms and their wooden extensions contrasting with the modern concrete edging. The joint line comes to an end at Burscough Bridge, but there is no longer a connection to the LO&P which it passes below.

Steamport

The first engine shed at Southport had been built by the LC&SR in 1848 and this was used by M&SR (L&YR) locomotives when the joint line opened from Burscough. The ELR on the other hand built their own shed near the station. After the amalgamation it was decided to concentrate all the locomotives on the former ELR shed, but it was not until 1871 that the shed was enlarged. A long

Above:
One of the major attractions for today's railway enthusiasts at Southport is the Steamport railway museum, housed in the ex-locomotive shed. Visiting 'Black 5' No 44932 is pictured at the museum on 3 November 1985 prior to working a special to Wigan Wallgate.
Brian Dobbs

Above:
Although photographed on 12 July 1950, Fairburn 2-6-4T No 2299 retains its LMS livery and number when pictured at Appley Bridge on the Southport-Wigan line.
Oliver F. Carter

Right:
Over 40 years there have been a number of subtle changes to Appley Bridge station: the platforms have been re-edged and resurfaced; new lighting has been installed; and, perhaps most significantly, the down platform shelter has been replaced with something more modest. The station is pictured on 22 May 1991 when Class 37/4 No 37430 stops with the 17.06 Manchester Victoria-Southport service. Unlike many other stations, however, Appley Bridge retains its attractive main station building on the up platform.
Paul D. Shannon

single-ended building containing six roads was designed by J. A. F. Aspinall and erected between Chapel Street and Central stations in 1891. It maintained a long but undistinguished career until closure in 1965, and gradually lapsed into dereliction before being acquired in 1971 with the view to forming the base for a working transport museum. In 1973 visitors got their first glimpse inside the shed as it moved nearer to restoration, but the formal opening of Steamport did not come until 1975.

The first locomotive to arrive on the site was a diesel shunter *Persil*, while the first steam engine was Peckett No 5 from Kidsgrove power station. In the mid-1970s the Liverpool Locomotive Group moved their collection to Southport, including the locomotives *Efficient* and *Lucy*. Today the museum

houses 14 steam engines and seven diesel locomotives, which includes an extensive collection of industrial locos. One of the more interesting exhibits is the ex-Mersey Railway 0-6-4T, No 5 *Cecil Raikes*, an engine of 1885 vintage fitted with condensing gear for working through the Mersey Tunnel. More recent BR additions include Class 03, 04 and 24 diesels, while the road vehicle collection comprises two ex-Southport buses, two trams and two steam traction engines. Of the original six roads in the shed, just five remain in use as no. 5 is now used to stable the road vehicles. Interestingly 1991 marked the centenary of the shed, as well as the 150th anniversary of the L&YR and to mark the event an L&YR 0-4-0ST 'Pug' was loaned to Steamport from its home base on the Worth Valley Railway.

4

The Preston & Wyre Railway

The Fleetwood Line

Due to the vision of Peter Hesketh-Fleetwood MP, the first railway to the Fylde Coast was promoted in 1835 as part of a scheme to create a new dock on the River Wyre. This area was part of the Hesketh Estate, and the development of a new port and a town linked to Preston (Maudland) by a 19-mile long railway was envisaged as a means to considerably enhance his fortunes. Yet there was another motive behind this grand aim, because in local terms there was no real reason for a railway or a port. At that time the Wyre estuary was just a huge area of sand dunes sparsely populated except for the small fishing communities, but this was also the period when the course of the main railway line to Scotland was being debated. So, once opened, the P&WR would become the northern terminus of the line from Euston, and steamships would be employed to complete the route to Ardrossan (for Glasgow).

The new town was called Fleetwood after its founder, and the work first began in May 1836. The railway was commenced around the same time, but the single track was not to open until July 1840, a full year after the amalgamation of the dock and railway companies. The Preston & Wyre had no stock of its own, and a leasing arrangement was made with the North Union Railway. At Fleetwood a steam ship offered a connection over Morecambe Bay to Bardsea (near Ulverston), forming a short cut in the route to the north. The importance of the harbour continued to grow, and by the end of 1841 sailings were being offered to Ardrossan, Belfast, Whitehaven and the Isle of Man. The advent of the Preston & Lancaster and later the Lancaster & Carlisle railways was to reduce the value of this maritime service to such an extent that it eventually ceased completely. However, for a while *this was* part of the main route to Scotland, and had the West Coast main line been taken round the Cumbrian coast as opposed to Shap, then the P&WR might still have formed an important link in the route north. Difficulties also existed in respect to the use of the port because it was a 'tidal' dock, and ships using the wharves risked being grounded at low water. Floating or 'wet' docks were proposed at an early stage, but all that happened was the dredging of the channel to form a deeper passage. While this situation continued, the size of vessels using Fleetwood would effectively remain limited to small coasters.

With the growing importance of the town, better rail links were essential, so in 1846 work was begun on doubling the line from Preston. The insecure timber trestle between Burn Naze and Fleetwood was closed, and opportunity was taken to deviate the section by the creation of a two-mile long embankment to carry the double track. By this time the L&YR had reached Preston via their share in the North Union Railway, and in July 1849 the Preston & Wyre (by then nearing bankruptcy) was jointly vested into the L&YR and the LNWR. With a proportionate ownership of two-thirds and one-third respectively, the line improvements were therefore paid for and completed by the joint owners and came into operation on 13 January 1851. In 1883 a new terminus was opened in Fleetwood, replacing the old station in Dock Street which was then closed.

After the L&YR/LNWR take-over the joint management committee effectively promoted the line, and the double track soon became inadequate for the traffic it was carrying and the section between Preston and Kirkham had to be quadrupled in 1889. A sharp curve at Poulton where the Blackpool branch diverged continued to give concern, and a

Below:
With substantial railway investment, the port of Fleetwood was developed into one of the major harbours on the northwest coast, as evidenced by this view of the Wyre Dock taken from the top of the grain elevator. It gives a good impression of the dockside railway in the mid-1920s, and the growing development of Fleetwood as a fishing port. Though the Grouping had taken place two years earlier, only a few wagons are lettered LMS and there is just one LNER example visible, the rest being L&YR, LNWR or Private Owner wagons — all the trawlers are from Fleetwood.
B. C. Lane Collection

Right:
Despite the fact that the port of Fleetwood still handles an exceptional level of traffic it is all road-borne and mostly loaded on to ships by the Ro-Ro principle. Sadly, no railway connections exist to the port even though the truncated stub of the P&WR is less than one mile away. However, visitors to the town might be misled into believing that there still is a station, as a modern road sign continues to point the way to the long closed terminus. Regretfully those intent on travelling by rail will be disappointed, as this view clearly reveals what has become of the passenger station which was adjacent to the passenger jetty.
Author

Right:
Poulton No 3 signal box pictured in 1896, at which date the box had 74 levers controlling a particularly complex junction.
B. C. Lane Collection

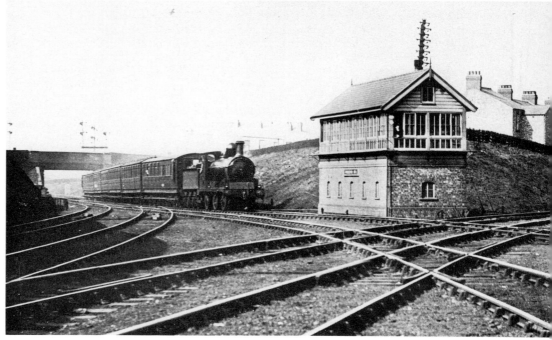

Below:
Although Poulton No 3 box remains intact, there has been a considerable amount of track rationalisation in the Poulton-le-Fylde area.
Class 47 No 47319 brings the 13.25 Burn Naze-Lindsey empties from the Fleetwood branch on to the Blackpool-Preston line at Poulton on 30 March 1989.
Paul D. Shannon

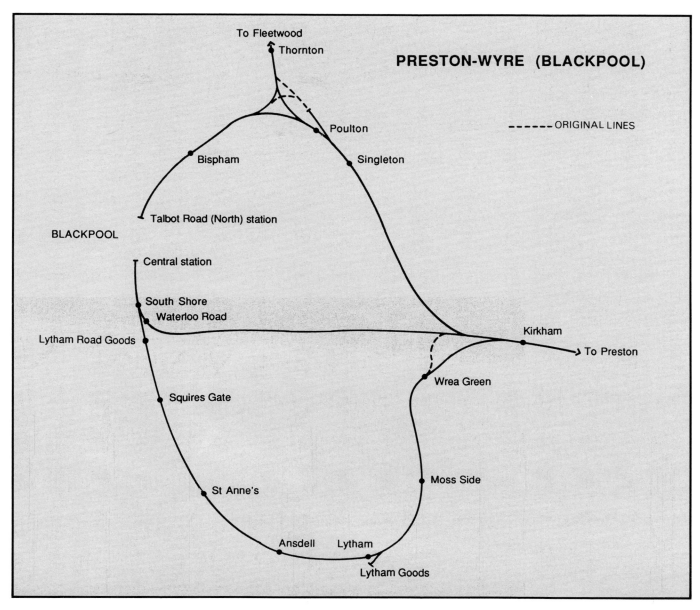

PRESTON-WYRE (BLACKPOOL)

------ ORIGINAL LINES

To Fleetwood
Thornton
Poulton
Bispham
Singleton
Talbot Road (North) station
BLACKPOOL
Central station
South Shore
Waterloo Road
Lytham Road Goods
Kirkham
To Preston
Wrea Green
Squires Gate
Moss Side
St Anne's
Ansdell   Lytham
Lytham Goods

decision was taken to improve the layout. Yet, before the work was begun, a serious derailment was experienced by an LNWR train to Stockport, which took the junction at high speed in July 1893. The improvements involved deviating the line between Poulton and Thornton, leaving only a short section to serve the old station for Poulton which became a goods depot. A more gentle curve led round to the Blackpool line and, in 1896, a new island station (with platforms of tremendous length) was provided for Poulton with the junction for Fleetwood just to the west of it. The construction of a curve from the Fleetwood line on to the Blackpool branch in 1899 allowed the commencement of a direct service between the two towns.

The Preston & Longridge Railway

The second railway project that involved Peter Hesketh-Fleetwood, was the Preston & Longridge Railway, which was promoted from Preston to Longridge Fell at the southern side of the Forest of Bowland. A substantial traffic in stone from the quarries on Longridge Fell had opened up during the 1830s, and to provide a convenient means of transport a 6½ mile horse-operated railway opened in May 1840.

The P&L was seen by the P&WR as a means to extend its line, and the Fleetwood, Preston & West Riding Junction Railway was authorised in July 1846, to promote a through route to Skipton. In November the P&WR leased the P&L, and work began on converting the line for locomotives and extending it to Maudland station in Preston in one direction and building a link from Grimsargh to Clitheroe in the other. However, by 1849 the railway was in such a critical financial state that a distress warrant was issued and the assets of the FP&WRJ seized. The P&L regained control of its line in 1852,

Right:

Class 50 No **418** at the unrebuilt Blackpool North on 19 August 1971 at the head of the 10.58 to Euston awaiting departure from one of the 'ordinary' station platforms. The station was reconstructed during 1973 and 1974, with the removal of the 'ordinary' platforms and the concentration of train services onto the remaining eight platforms of the 'excursion' side. The work also included the adaptation of the 1938-built concourse. In 1973, Blackpool North handled over 1.8 million passengers; 139,000 of them arrived in 444 excursion trains.
R. E. Ruffell

With the twin train-shed roof in the background, the 'excursion' platforms at Blackpool North are doing good business. The long 1938-built concourse is clearly visible.
Ian Allan Library

Below:

The dramatic changes wrought at Blackpool North during the 1973-74 reconstruction are clearly visible in this shot. The removal of the twin train-shed has allowed a much clearer view of the famous Blackpool Tower, whilst in the foreground a Class 37 waits to depart with a passenger service on 17 June 1992.
Gavin Morrison

Left:
After rebuilding, Blackpool North assumed the role of the main station for Blackpool, and as such it still retains adequate platform accommodation to service both local and excursion traffic. In the summer season a variety of locomotive and coaching stock types are to be seen, but today this includes few of the BR Mk 1 examples which predominate in this 1987 view. On 3 September No 37121 approaches Blackpool North with 09.21 from Sheffield, while a Class 08 shunter stands at the carriage sidings neck.
Paul D. Shannon

Left:
Lytham station, the former terminus of the old B&LR, seen around the turn of the 19th century, as No 979, one of the 6ft 3in four-coupled passenger locomotives, blows off steam whilst waiting with a van train. Though the lines throughout the Fylde area were jointly owned with the LNWR, they were largely viewed as L&YR territory as Crewe had only a 33% stake in their acquisition. Until recently visitors to Lytham could have visited the Motive Power Museum in Dock Road, where a collection of industrial locomotives and aircraft were on display. Unfortunately, the museum has now closed and the collection has been dispersed.
Bucknall Collection/Ian Allan Library

Left:
As this view of Pleasure Beach station (complete with a Class 142 arriving from Blackburn) shows, the south line has been reduced to nothing more than a long single siding. Running all the way from Kirkham to a pair of buffer stops at Blackpool South, the line is now a very basic affair, though the pseudo-Victorian edifice erected to service the Pleasure Beach does look quite attractive apart from the footbridge.
Martin Eltham

but in 1856 the FP&WRJ was reformed and it purchased the P&L for £48,000. Though the title of the company still implied the desire to carry on through to Yorkshire, the Clitheroe extension was dropped for all time. Towards the end of 1856 a branch passenger service was started, but this only lasted until 1930. However, the private railway to the asylum at Wittingham still provided a service from Grimsargh until 1957 when the branch closed. Today a truncated stub of the old P&L still remains, but it only runs to serve the coal concentration depot in the Preston suburb of Deepdale.

The Blackpool Branch

It is hard to imagine Blackpool as anything but a raucous holiday spot, teeming with life from early morning to the early hours, yet when the P&WR was constructed it was little more than a rabbit warren among the sand dunes, the black pool being a peat bog which drained into the sea roughly where the central pier now stands. A tourist traffic of sorts had been developing since the late-18th century, and the P&WR ran special excursions to Fleetwood with connecting horse-drawn vans from Poulton to Blackpool. Work on the 3½ mile branch to Blackpool began in November 1846 and was completed in the astonishing time of just four months. The single track branch left the Fleetwood line at Poulton and terminated in Talbot Square, where a grand station façade fronted a collection of rather mean buildings and offices. A considerable amount of spoil from the construction sites was carted down to the developing promenade and tipped into the sea, where the resulting promontory was to later form the entrance for the North Pier. The doubling of the branch was considered in 1856 and again 1864, but work was not fully completed until 1865-67 though a new station had been provided for Bispham in 1857.

The problems of the Poulton junction have already been mentioned in the preceding section, but this was just part of the Blackpool branch improvements in the 1890s. Station improvements at Talbot Road between 1896-98 culminated in a six platform general section covered by an overall roof, supplemented by a larger 'excursion' section with long bays for the seasonal traffic. Talbot Road remained the principal station until the 'direct' (or Marton) line opened in 1903, when Central began to assume the more dominant role. Talbot Road was eventually re-named Blackpool North by the LMS in the early 1930s.

Blackpool Central

At the same time as the P&WR were promoting their Blackpool branch, they were aiming a second line to Lytham on the southern curve of the Fylde Coast. Diverging at Kirkham, a 4¾-mile long single track branch was commenced at the end of July 1845. Like its northern counterpart, the work was speedily undertaken and it opened on 17 February 1846. Intermediate stations were provided at Wrea Green and Moss Side, with a further station at Warton opening in 1865. The increasing popularity of Blackpool and

Station, St. Annes-on-Sea.

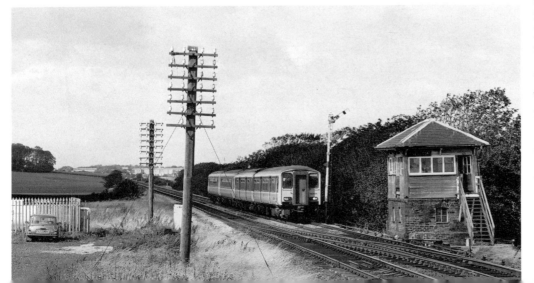

Left:
The rationalisation of the line south from Blackpool also coincided with the demise of the Blackpool South-Kirkham direct line, which was closed on 7 September **1964**. The desolation of the once important station at Blackpool South, seen on 14 April **1982**, tells its own story. Beyond the station, the weed-strewn trackbed leads on to Central.
John Glover

Left:
The modern and rationalised Blackpool South; a single platform with basic shelter where once expresses used to pass. A Network NorthWest-liveried Class 142 awaits departure for Colne from the new station.
Author

Below left:
While the southern and central exits from Blackpool have been severely ravaged in the past three decades, the passenger service to Blackpool North remains quite intensive. Most of the workings have now been 'Sprinterised', but a fast and relatively efficient passenger carrying service has been maintained even though it is put under extreme pressure at peak times. Running local trains beyond Preston has helped considerably, but the combination of different types of DMUs on some journeys tend to make for a bouncy ride. One such mixture is pictured at Singleton on 3 September **1990**, with Class 150 and 156 sets making up the 13.57 for Stockport.
Paul D. Shannon

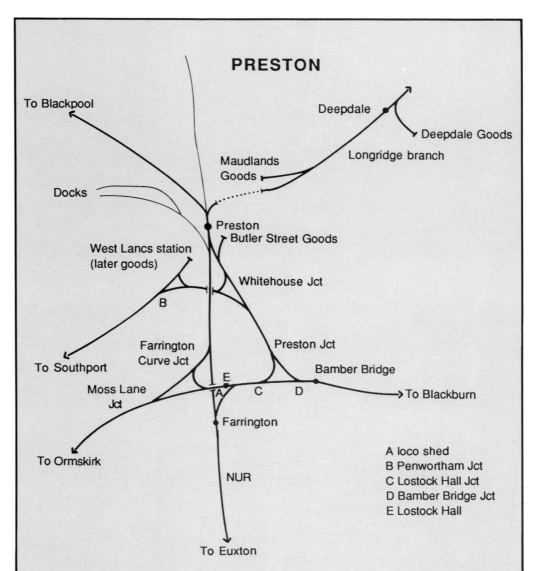

PRESTON

To Blackpool

Deepdale

Deepdale Goods

Maudlands Goods

Longridge branch

Docks

Preston

Butler Street Goods

West Lancs station
(later goods)

Whitehouse Jct

B

Preston Jct

To Southport

Farrington
Curve Jct

Bamber Bridge

E

Moss Lane
Jct

TA   C   D

To Blackburn

Farrington

NUR

A loco shed
B Penwortham Jct
C Lostock Hall Jct
D Bamber Bridge Jct
E Lostock Hall

To Ormskirk

To Euxton

Below:
The Preston & Longridge Railway was a testament to the false ambition of the second era of railway mania, and the grandiose scheme to extend the line into Yorkshire never materialised. When passenger services were withdrawn in 1930 it was destined to remain as a freight line for a further three decades, though the last working was an RCTS railtour in September 1962. Some 10 years earlier ex-L&YR 0-6-0 No 52182 is pictured shunting at the terminus as a Ribble Motor Services Leyland Titan PD2 runs over the level crossing.
W. G. Aspell

Left:
Today just a very short truncated stub of the P&LR remains, running down to Deepdale to serve the coal concentration depot located there. The line has been reduced to a single track and the ballast has become the dumping ground for local rubbish. A rusted wheelbarrow, an old dustbin and the proverbial plastic traffic cones are some of the more noticeable items pictured alongside No 56075 as it heads along the branch.
Paul D. Shannon

Centre left:
From the outset the L&YR were dependent on running powers to operate through Preston and for joint use of the station there. It has to be said, however, that they were not always on the best of terms with their neighbours the LNWR. Despite this, co-operation did exist in several forms, notably the jointly run Park Hotel (which opened near to the station in **1882** and remained in railway ownership until **1949**). In this quiet scene an Aspinall 2-4-2T stands on the middle road between Platforms Nos 2 and 3; locomotive apart, it is a scene not greatly changed even today.
Bucknall Collection/Ian Allan Library

Below left:
The interior of the modern Preston station on **17 June 1992** with Class **142** No **142024** awaiting departure from platform 2. Although the building has been reroofed, there are a number of detail points that enable a direct comparison to be made. *Gavin Morrison*

Lytham as watering places ensured the development of the stretch of coast between the two towns, and it became logical to build a connecting railway. This project was undertaken by the Blackpool & Lytham Railway, an organisation which proved it was completely divorced from the P&WR by having no physical connection with it at either end. The first sod was cut in September 1861 and work was completed a year later. However, as the primary business of the B&L was tourist-orientated there was no point in opening until the following spring. There was just one intermediate station at South Shore, as the resort of St Anne's-on-Sea did not exist then. It was intended to carry the line forward from Lytham over the Ribble Estuary, and thus to Preston but this was never achieved. In the period between 1868-73 additional stations were opened at Stony Hill, Cross Slack and Ansdell - but Stony Hill was poorly supported and closed as early as 1872. Cross Slack became St Anne's in 1875, as the new resort started to grow in importance.

The B&L maintained its independence up to 1871 when it was absorbed by the L&YR/LNWR and vested into the P&WR. At the same time a connecting line between the two railways at Lytham was authorised. Simultaneous with the opening of the connection on 1 July 1874, a new line was opened between Wrea Green and Kirkham, shortening the route to Preston. Prompted by dissatisfaction with L&YR services, Blackpool Town Council considered building its own line to Preston during the mid-1870s, and out of this was born the Blackpool Railway. In association with the Manchester, Sheffield & Lincolnshire, it envisaged a line to connect Lytham with the West Lancashire Railway,

which ran from Southport to Preston. The scheme for a direct line from Lytham to Preston re-emerged several times in the late-1880s, but it again failed to come to fruition. From 1878 onwards, the former B&L terminus at Blackpool became known as the Central Station, but as time progressed it was quickly outgrown and considerable enlargement was approved. The work was completed by Easter 1901, when a new station with six covered and eight excursion platforms opened.

The rather circuitous routes taken by both lines into Blackpool continued to give substance to the demands for a more direct line, and in 1896 a joint Act authorised the construction of the 6¾ mile 'Marton' line from Kirkham to a point just north of South Shore. A new junction was planned at Kirkham, with use being made of a single-line fly-over. The new line, and the widened section from South Shore to Central, opened in the spring of 1903. The 'Marton' line had just one intermediate station, at Waterloo Road, just 300yd from South Shore. This arrangement was very inconvenient, and within a few years it was decided to combine both stations. In 1914 a tender was issued to convert Waterloo Road to serve both lines, but due to the advent of World War 1 this work was not completed until July 1916 when South Shore closed and the new station took its name. Perhaps the final development was the opening of Squire's Gate station in 1931, which was erected on a site near to the former Stony Hill station.

Into Decline

As the P&WR moved into the 20th century it was enjoying a high level of traffic in passengers, a trend which continued through to the end of World War 2. Fleetwood saw several changes, the main one being the withdrawal of the Belfast steamer service in 1928 when the LMS transferred the sailings on to the ex-MR route via Heysham. In the early 1940s, the redundant grain elevator at Fleetwood was completely demolished. In 1966 the decision was taken to terminate all trains at the former Wyre Dock station, which was renamed Fleetwood when the former terminus was abandoned. However, this was short lived and in April 1970 (just before the holiday season), BR withdrew the passenger service and closed the line down to the docks and today the freight-only line terminates just three-quarters of a mile from Wyre Dock.

Blackpool traffic remained fairly constant up to the late 1950s, and despite a noticeable decline still brought a heavy seasonal flow into all three stations. Yet the tactic adopted by Beeching and British Railways has to be one of the most astonishing of all time. Quite without any good reason they announced that the Central station and the South loco shed would be closed at the end of the 1964 sum-

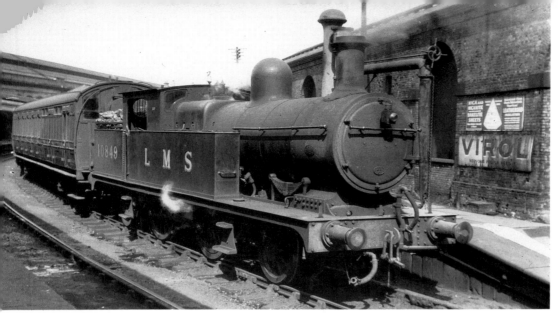

Above left:

In the last year before Nationalisation, ex-L&YR 2-4-2T No 10849 awaits departure from Preston with a train for Southport. Originally numbered 674 by the L&YR, No 10849 was one of a handful of the class to be rebuilt with Belpaire firebox and extended smokebox. The locomotive was withdrawn in February 1950, never having received its British Railways number.
B. C. Lane Collection

Left:

The ex-L&YR side of the joint station has been completely obliterated to provide car parking spaces. The exterior wall of the surviving station building provides the reference point.
Gavin Morrison

Bottom left:

To illustrate the decline of railways in the Fylde area, we might look at the changing traffic patterns witnessed in the past century. A specific example might be the club trains which ran from January 1896 onwards. Despite the difficult course of the 42 miles to Manchester, these trains had a booked time from Lytham of just one hour. Early in the LMS era, an unidentified Hughes 4-6-0 heads the Manchester-Blackpool club express. Though the train carried ordinary commuters, membership to the special club car was a prestigious honour, numbers were limited and a strict code of ethics applied — including the rule that 'no member shall open any window in the club saloon car'.
B. C. Lane Collection

mer season. Thereafter, all traffic would terminate at the South station, whilst the direct line would be retained for summer traffic only. In February 1964, Blackpool North shed closed, ostensibly for good, but it was reopened in November after the closure of the Central shed, and appears to have seen intermittent use until early in 1968. The Blackpool-Fleetwood trains were also withdrawn at the end of 1964, but their value was dubious as the route had long been duplicated by the more direct tram service.

Thereafter a new traffic pattern emerged for Blackpool, with trains from east Lancashire, Yorkshire and the north running into the North station and those from Manchester and the south running into Blackpool South. Regretfully even this half-cocked arrangement did not last long and the direct, most convenient, route was subsequently closed. Central became a bingo hall and amusement arcade, whilst its platforms were levelled and reduced to the status of a rather tatty car park. Today the route via Lytham is just a glorified siding running from Kirkham to Blackpool South. Finally, Blackpool North was up-graded, made the town's principal station, and completely re-built in 1974 but further away from the town centre on the site of the original 'excursion' platforms.

The Preston & Wyre in the 1990s

After leaving Preston the electric overhead wires continue along the former Preston & Wyre for a short distance, intimating that the scheme for electrifying the line to Blackpool North remains a long term and realistic ambition. Just before Salwick station, a private delivery siding serves the British Nuclear Fuels plant. At Kirkham, most of the station buildings are still intact though the canopy has been removed. The massive North cabin is still operational, but it will probably vanish when the line is resignalled and comes under Preston Power Box. The junction at Kirkham still maintains a number of sidings, all of which are associated with the Chief Civil Engineer's Department. Little remains of the Marton line, except a short stub of track running towards the CE Tip at Kirkham, beyond which a long section of the line's trackbed forms part of the M55 motorway.

The line to Blackpool South passes through some lovely countryside, but the stations at Moss Side and Lytham are rather bland and unappealing. By way of contrast, someone has taken a considerable amount of trouble at Ansdell & Fairhaven where the single face of the old island platform has a very neat appearance and is furnished with flowers. St Anne's-on-Sea, despite being staffed, gets my vote for being the most rundown station in Lancashire, for it really is rather awful and only comes a close second behind Halifax as the worst ex-L&YR station today. The old down line still retains some of its facilities along with a modernised booking hall, but it is the opposite side which seriously affects the view. The Preston-bound platform has been chopped in half, and its buildings are completely derelict. The canopy is still intact, but it is in a pretty awful state — surely this once-attractive shelter must be of interest to some preservation society.

Squires Gate, with the airport close by, is just a very basic halt with only a short section of one platform in use. A more recent addition is the new station serving the Pleasure

Beach, its modern wooden platform furnished with a very attractive canopy built in a traditional style. Finally the train draws into Blackpool South, a single platform with little more than notice boards and a bus-shelter waiting area. Poor compensation for what once stood on this site. The remainder of the area, like Central, has been taken over for a car park. Beyond South Station, a few reminders can be found that the Blackpool & Lytham once ran into the centre of the town.

From Kirkham the old main line runs north to Poulton, but the intermediate station at Singleton has now been closed for 60 years. Poulton's island platform is overgrown towards the ends, but the central section retains its L&YR canopy, red-brick buildings, original clock, and is pleasantly furnished with floral hanging baskets. The line to Blackpool North curves round to the southwest, and, apart from the intermediate station at Layton (renamed from Bispham in 1938), little is encountered until the massive carriage siding complex on the approach to Blackpool North.

Poulton No 3 Box controls the junction for the freight-only line to Burn Naze, which becomes single track just beyond Poulton. This passes through the site of the old Thornton station to Burn Naze where a couple of industrial sidings diverge. It then commences the last leg, to the ICI's Hillhouse Works at Thornton and up to the power station site. Though the line still carries a number of freight trains, it is singularly ineffective at capturing the potentially huge level of traffic that could be sent this way as it terminates short of any purposeful objective as far as the port is concerned. Given the current attitude over developing freight lines, perhaps the best that could be hoped for is the thought that it would make an ideal base for a preserved steam railway. However, in Fleetwood there stands an enduring monument to the grand plans of the P&WR in the shape of the former railway-owned hotel, which still bears a name that proclaims it was the one-time terminus of the WCML – The North Euston!

5

The East Lancashire Railway

The Manchester, Bury & Rossendale Railway was formed in October 1843 with the intention of promoting a line from the Manchester & Bolton Railway at Clifton Junction to Ramsbottom and Rawtenstall in the Rossendale Valley. In so doing the line would link a number of growing cotton-spinning towns to Manchester, and also enjoy considerable levels of coal and stone traffic. The company was authorised in 1844, and the headquarters were established adjacent to the Bolton Street station in Bury. North of Bury the line was proposed as a single track, but with the promotion of the Blackburn, Burnley, Accrington & Colne Extension Railway it was decided to build the line double through to Stubbins Junction.

The two rather cumbersome titles were clearly unsuitable, so the more apt East Lancashire Railway was adopted from November 1844 onwards. This name was authorised by an Act of Parliament the following July, and 12 months later powers were granted to extend from Lower Booths at Rawtenstall to Bacup. A feature of the railway was the difficult terrain it encountered, and from Clifton Junction the line was to cross and re-cross the River Irwell several times during its travels north (this section is also detailed in Chapter 6). Beyond Bury the line passed through two tunnels, at Brooksbottom and Nutall, before attaining Ramsbottom station and thence via Stubbins to Rawtenstall. The 14 miles from Clifton Junction, which included no less than 12 crossings of the Irwell, opened in September 1845 amid great celebration. Intermediate stations were at Radcliffe Bridge, Bury, Summerseat and Ramsbottom, but not all were complete at the time of opening. Additional facilities were provided at Molyneux Brow (1853), Ringley Road (1847) and Clifton Junction (1846-47).

The extension was even more difficult to build, and work was separated into three sections: Stubbins-Accrington, and from Accrington to Colne and to Blackburn. A series of viaducts and a 146yd-long tunnel at Haslingden were required for the single track line as it climbed to a summit at Baxenden, where wide expanses of peat bogs were encountered. The summit of the line was particularly hard to achieve as the depth of the peat was

Right:
When the ELR line opened from Bury in 1845 it made a junction with the Bolton line at Clifton, and a station opened there the following year. Looking from the Bolton end of the station towards Manchester, the Bury platforms are seen on the far left, with the LNWR line from Patricroft intersecting them at a lower level. Today only a basic station is left on the Bolton line and the once busy junction has ceased to exist. Until 1987 a spur came in at nearby Agecroft. This had allowed stopping trains to loop on to the Atherton line and call at Pendleton (Broad Street), a service 'guaranteed' by BR when they posted closure notices for Pendleton Old in 1966.
B. C. Lane Collection

Right:
Now reduced to simply a station on the Manchester-Bolton line and shorn of its 'Junction' suffix, Clifton lost the ex-L&YR route north to Bury on 5 December 1966 and the ex-LNWR line south to Patricroft has also disappeared. Seen in June 1992, the station has had its original buildings replaced by bus shelter-type structures and its gas lighting by modern electric lights.
Gavin Morrison

Right:
Accrington was the junction with the line south to Stubbins Junction. When pictured here on 23 June 1962, the station was largely unmodernised. A Preston-bound DMU forms the 4.18pm departure from Todmorden. On the extreme right can be seen a train at the Stubbins Junction-side platforms.
I. G. Holt

around 20ft and, in order to drive out the water, boulders and rock had to be dumped into the treacle-like morass. For three months the dumping of stone continued, before the track-bed became stable enough to carry a line of rails.

The descent to Accrington was down the Baxenden Bank, a line which descended on a ruling gradient of 1 in 40 and required some pretty demanding work from the drivers on this section. Understandably the foot of the bank was the location where the L&YR installed its first sand drags. There were only three intermediate stations: at Helmshore, Haslingden and Baxenden. Accrington lay just beyond the foot of the bank, with its tri-angular layout resulting in very tightly curved station platforms. This was a particular problem for those Colne trains which slipped coaches here; these had to approach the station braking hard enough to slow down for the 5mph limit over the viaduct beyond, but still being able to re-establish sufficient vacuum in the train pipe to allow the slip portion's guard his reserve braking power. The Manchester-Colne non-stop service was well patronised, and on several days of the week Accrington had its own separate working following hard on the heels of the Colne express.

After World War 2 services north of Bury were badly curtailed, and Baxenden was the first passenger casualty in 1951 followed by Haslingden in 1960, but the line remained as a major through route until 1961. Though most of north Lancashire services were then routed via Blackburn/Bolton and Bury/Radcliffe, a few trains still used the electric route via Prestwich. But this still provided a basic hourly service through Accrington, until the autumn of 1964 when the Colne-Manchester service was cut back dramatically, and largely reduced to an Accrington-Bury DMU working. Even this was not to continue, and on

3 December 1966 (a time when shoppers were packing trains to capacity) the service was withdrawn between Accrington and Bury and the section down to Stubbins closed. Today part of the track-bed north of Stubbins forms a nature trail, whilst other parts have now been taken over for the A56(T).

Accrington-Blackburn

When the Stubbins-Accrington line began on 17 August 1848, the Accrington-Blackburn section was already in operation, having opened two months earlier on 19 June. There were several engineering works, but the three principal ones were a 434yd-long tunnel east of Blackburn and two huge timber trestles: the first of these crossed the Rishton Reservoir and the other spanned the Aspen valley, where the ground was too soft to support masonry piers. The 5¼ mile-long section passed through attractive countryside, roughly duplicating the course of the Leeds-Liverpool Canal which had opened in 1816. Though there is little of significance in this section of railway, it formed a vital part of the link over the northern part of east Lancashire. The viaducts at Rishton and across the Aspen Valley were turned into embankments, but the latter took a considerable period of time to achieve. Work commenced in 1891, but was suspended sometime later and only fully resumed at the end of World War 1.

Today the line forms a well-used route across north Lancashire and at Blackburn the station yard still has a number of sidings, most of which tend to be occupied by cement wagons these days, a far cry from the wagon loads of cotton which once stood on the same roads. On the outskirts of the station Daisyfield West Junction still exists to carry the line north to Hellifield, though regrettably not currently used for a regular passenger service. Further east Great Harwood Junction once marked the commencement of the North

Below left:
By 1982 Accrington station had been much reduced. The facilities on the westbound platform had been replaced by a much more basic structure, the bay had been removed and the station had had improved lighting installed. A DMU, headed by No 50466, arrives at the station with the 10.29 Preston-Colne service.
D. T. Roberts

Below:
Since the closure of the line to Stubbins Junction, Accrington station has gone into severe decline. Today it is little more than an eyesore, the cut-back footbridge and the solitary brick building on the Colne-bound platform do little to enhance its appearance, although there is evidence of investment in the new station building on platform one. Most of the Blackburn-bound side has become weed-strewn and neglected, whilst the Bury platforms have been totally removed and their site is now occupied by an industrial estate. On 29 August 1991 No 142052 stops with a Preston-Colne service, while a number of 'Rovers' supporters wait on the opposite platform for a train to take them to Blackburn and the first home match of the season.
Graham S. Yeadon.

The third leg of the ELR was east to Burnley, from where the line would then curve north to Colne. The major construction on this line was the 21-arch viaduct immediately east of Accrington station, and this was to prove an immediate obstacle due to problems encountered with subsidence. Though much of the first structure was demolished and rebuilt before the line opened, by 1866 it had become unsafe again and required rebuilding. The work was reported complete by September 1867, when the new 's' shaped structure commenced carrying traffic. The line opened to Burnley Barracks in September 1848, but problems with the viaduct on the approach to Burnley Bank Top station delayed the opening of the next section until December.

With this complete, the ELR had reached Burnley 11 months ahead of the L&YR branch from Todmorden. When the L&YR line opened in September 1850 it terminated at Thorneybank, but in a rare example of co-operation, the two companies agreed to the provision of a connection between the ELR at Gannow and the L&YR branch which opened in September 1850. Meanwhile the ELR had forged onto Colne, but not without some considerable difficulties with their contractor. They finally achieved the junction with the Midland branch in February 1849, though the line from Skipton had opened some months earlier. From Accrington the stations were Huncoat, Hapton, and Rose Grove (for Padiham), followed by the two Burnley stations, after which came Marsden (later Brierfield) and Nelson.

From its outset the ELR was a considerable thorn in the L&YR's flesh, and the problems

Above:

The small intermediate station of Rishton is still open between Accrington and Blackburn, but its facilities are very basic with bus-shelter type waiting areas and bleak platforms — a far cry from this pre-World War 1 view of Rishton with its substantial station buildings, covered footbridge, large goods warehouse and a yard packed full of vans and wagons.
B. C. Lane Collection

Below right:

The station at Blackburn has seen some alteration since L&YR days, particularly after it was 'modernised' in the early 1970s, but its interior still maintains a very traditional 'Lanky' appearance beneath the overall roof. Next to Huddersfield it has the distinction of being one of the finest large stations surviving on the old L&YR system today. It has two island platforms and associated bays, but the island on the south side has been considerably shortened and only one face is still in use, and then only as a relief platform. On 6 April 1990 No 37058 starts from the station yard with 11.30 steel empties working to Lackenby.
Paul D. Shannon

Lancashire loop, but the western end has long been devoid of tracks, with only the section from Padiham power station to Rose Grove being retained. On the direct line between Blackburn and Accrington the two intermediate stations at Rishton and Church & Oswaldtwistle, once well used and attractively kept, are still open but now reduced to just very basic affairs. The final section includes the approach to Accrington where a massive engine shed complex once dominated the scene, but its allocation of steam locomotives was transferred to Rose Grove in 1961 and it became a DMU depot, though even that has now been swept away.

were manifest in many different ways. Yet by 1851 the first mention of an amalgamation began to appear in the railway press, but no progress was made in this direction until 1854 due to the opposition of the Midland Railway. At the end of 1856 the terms had been settled, but once again the Midland (assisted by the LNWR) managed to delay Parliamentary authorisation for the amalgamation until 13 August 1859. At this time the assets of the ELR, valued at almost £3½ million, were united with the L&YR, along with the three jointly owned lines (Blackburn, Clifton Junc-Salford, and Burscough-Southport). As a further consequence of the amalgamation some rationalisation was undertaken, and the most

significant step was the closure of Thorney-bank in November 1866 and the provision of a new L&YR station at Manchester Road.

After this period the main services were basically aimed at providing an east-west link from Preston to Yorkshire via Todmorden, and a north-south route from Colne to Manchester. Connections were made at Rose Grove and Accrington, whilst Blackburn provided another useful interchange once the Hellifield line services began. The peak or through trains from Colne were well patronised, but the intermediate services were causing some concern due to the competing tram service between Burnley and Colne. The trains got progressively smaller until they

Right:
The North Lancashire loop ran through Great Harwood, Simonstone (pictured here) and Padiham, before rejoining the Burnley line just before Rose Grove. It was a difficult line to construct as it encountered very hilly countryside in the valley of Lancashire's River Calder. Its opening, therefore, was accomplished in progressive stages. The line from Rose Grove to Padiham opened to goods in July 1875, with passenger trains starting 14 months later. However, the through service to Blackburn did not begin until 15 October 1877.
Barry C. Lane Collection

Below right:
The 10-mile loop was severely graded, and the steepest section was a 1 in 40 incline between Padiham and Rose Grove. Therefore it was used mainly by local trains until these were withdrawn in December 1957. Goods services remained in operation until November 1964, when the section from Blackburn to Padiham closed. At the time of writing a Workington-Padiham coal working has been introduced to eliminate the previous road-haulage of coal for the power station — however, in recent years traffic on the branch has been more commonly associated with oil trains such as No 47369 seen arriving with loaded oil tanks in February 1991.
Paul D. Shannon

comprised just one or two coaches, so the L&YR took the decision to introduce railmotor operation on the off-peak workings and provision was made for the new service by the construction of halts at Bott Lane, Reedley Hallows and New Hall Bridge. The Colne service had been allocated a permanent railmotor from September 1906, and except for a few breaks they continued on this working up to the early 1930s. However, at an early stage it had been extended through Burnley to Rose Grove in order to provide a more convenient connection for passengers travelling beyond Burnley. With the demise of the railmotors, the LMS reverted to using ex-L&YR 2-4-2Ts, several of which were converted to push-pull operation and coupled to one or two ex-railmotor trailers. As these trailers were already fitted with vacuum controls for driver operation, they were used with great advantage well into BR days when DMUs were introduced.

The through coaches from Colne to Euston were 'temporarily' withdrawn to allow the Manchester-Crewe electrification to take place, but they were never to be restored. Further curtailment of the DMU workings led to the establishment of what was a basic service from Colne to Manchester and Preston, but after December 1966 the Manchester trains ceased. The line from Skipton seemed assured as both Beeching and the 1967 'White Paper' appeared to leave it alone, yet, at the end of 1968 it was announced that no subsidy would be forthcoming to guarantee this link from Lancashire into Yorkshire. Its closure was rushed through with an astonishing speed, and the last train ran on 31 January 1970. Colne station, with its distinctive Midland architecture then became the terminus of a long L&YR branch line, and it has continued to decline ever since.

Up to 1986 the section from Rose Grove to just north of Nelson had remained furnished with double track, but today the entire line to Colne is just a long siding with a few basic stations stuck on it. However, despite its lack of architectural merit it is well worth travelling for the scenery alone. Boarding the DMU (invariably a Class 142) at Colne's bare single platform, the train heads out for Nelson station which is similarly depressing. Pretty countryside makes up for things, until the train curves into Burnley Central station (renamed from Bank Top in 1944). Though the station buildings are both modern and comprehensive, they serve only a single platform. Nearby the signal box is derelict, whilst the former sidings were bulldozed level in the summer of 1991. Burnley Barracks is also a single platform, located in a deep cutting and looking rather unsavoury despite its recent modernisation.

After Gannow Junction, the once extensive island station at Rose Grove is just a shadow of its former self. Though it was an important exchange station, and still serves this function to a lesser degree today, the buildings have

been replaced by a rather draughty bus-shelter type waiting area. As for the huge goods yard and the engine shed (one of BR's last three steam depots) they have all been swept away, and the station is now dominated by the recently constructed M65 motorway which begins to run alongside the line at this point. Next comes Rose Grove Junction, where the remaining stub of the old North Lancashire Loop diverges, still used to carry the occasional oil train to the power station at Padiham. Finally, as the line follows the course of the motorway towards Accrington two very basic stations are served at Hapton and Huncoat.

The Blackburn & Preston Railway

First projected in 1843, the Blackburn & Preston Railway was commenced on 20 August 1844, when the first sod was cut

Below left:
The Aspen viaduct was one of the most substantial feats of civil engineering on the old ELR, and in addition to spanning the valley with a railway line, it also carried a walkway on its side. Timber viaducts were fine in the earlier days of railways — cheaper to construct than stone and easier to widen when lines required doubling. However, they were unable to handle the increasing loads satisfactorily as locomotives and trains got larger. Timber also suffered rapid deterioration, particularly around the joints, and at Aspen substantial reconstruction had to be undertaken in the mid-1880s due to a combination of these factors. So, by the end of the century, powers had been obtained to fill in the viaduct and create an embankment, but this work appears to have taken some years to complete.
B. C. Lane Collection

Below left:
Over the years the important junctions at Farrington have been a fascinating place for railway enthusiasts. One of the most curious sights was the Blackpool trains coming from the north. These would come whistling down through Preston and on to the old ELR line, then screech through Preston Junction and Lostock Hall, cross the main line and then rejoin it at Farrington West, before beetling back off through Preston and on to the Blackpool line — all to avoid a reversal. Though much reduced in size, a large variety of locomotives still pass through Farrington, and on 3 September 1990 No 31233 takes the Lostock Hall spur at Farrington Junction with the 7E34 Ashton in Makerfield-Lindsey bitumen empties.
Paul D. Shannon

Right:
The strategic importance of
Lower Darwen can be
illustrated by the fact that
this was the location where
the L&YR chose to erect an
engine shed to serve the
Blackburn area. Eight roads
were provided, and even late
in the LMS era upwards of 40
engines were allocated to the
depot — mostly goods types.
By way of contrast the
passenger station was a
much smaller affair and, as
this view shows, rather
limited in its facilities. Of
particular interest is the low
height of the platforms and
the neatly raked ash ballast.
B. C. Lane Collection

Below right:
With the surviving piers of
the overbridge as a reference
point, it is clear that little
remains to remind today's
passengers that there was
once a station at Lower
Darwen. Whilst the majority
of stations survive on the
now singled Bolton-
Blackburn line, Lower
Darwen was not so fortunate.
It closed on 3 November
1958. The site is seen on
17 June 1992. *Gavin Morrison*

near Hoghton. It was to take just 22 months to build, despite requiring substantial engineering and massive viaducts over the River Darwen. In April 1845 the problem of access to Preston was raised, with the B&P agreeing to pay the North Union a toll to use their line from Farrington into Preston. The engineer favoured a direct route into the town, but the directors were keen to make a junction with the Liverpool, Ormskirk & Preston Railway in order to provide a through route to Liverpool — an objective which, in view of the considerable supplies of raw cotton that came into East Lancashire, is hardly surprising. Even so, for the first year the line only handled passenger traffic after it opened on 1 June 1846. To cater for this four stations were erected between Preston and Blackburn, these being at Cherry Tree, Hoghton, Pleas-ington, and Bamber Bridge — with a further station being provided at Mill Hill in 1887.

Amalgamation with the East Lancashire Railway took place just two months after opening, but this prospect had been on the cards for over a year. Thereafter the issue of a direct line into Preston was once again raised, and this time it was pursued by the directors who obtained an Act to build the cut-off route from Bamber Bridge to Preston in 1847. Though this Act was opposed by Preston Corporation, the shorter route opened in the autumn of 1850 allowing the connection at Farrington to be abandoned. Trains from the LO&P route were provided with a spur from Lostock Hall to Preston Junction, and thus no longer had to reverse to join the NUR at Farrington. Further development of the B&P came in the form of

Left:
Bolton was one of the most important stations on the old L&YR network, with routes radiating north towards Blackburn, east to Bury, south to Manchester and west towards Wigan, and this importance was reflected in the scale of the station. Unlike many other towns on the ex-L&YR system, Bolton has retained many of its rail links; the only major casualty being the line to Bury and Rochdale, which closed on 5 October 1970. The scale of the station is reflected in this shot, taken as late as 30 May 1985, with Class 45 No 45077 heading the 09.57 Appley Bridge-Dean Lane Greater Manchester Council refuse train through the town.
Paul D. Shannon

Left:
A lot has changed at Bolton in five years. The station layout has been rationalised and colour light signalling has been installed. Although the platform canopies remain (indeed one has been repainted), the main station buildings in Trinity Street were demolished in 1987 as part of a £4.5 million scheme to build a bus/rail interchange at the station. By 1990, the 'Peaks' are also a thing of the past as Class 31 No 31412 heads the 09.08 Barrow-Manchester Victoria southwards out of the station. The train was loco-hauled as part of the contingency plans produced as a result of difficulties with the introduction of the Class 158s.
Tom Clift

piecemeal additions, the first being a 528yd-long branch curving off to serve a coal depot in Blackburn which opened in September 1848. The Lancashire Union Railway, which provided a direct (but very steep) route between Chorley and Blackburn opened towards the end of 1869, with intermediate stations at Heapy, Brinscall, Withnell and Feniscowles before joining the B&D at Cherry Tree.

At Preston Junction a new station was opened in 1852, but a major building programme of the 1880s was to affect the entire southern approach to Preston. Motive power facilities in the area had been a matter of concern to the loco-department, and they had repeatedly requested the provision of an engine shed so that they could get their engines out of the shed shared with the LNWR. This ambition was realised in 1882, when the modern eight-road Lostock Hall shed was erected to the west of Watkins Lane in the 'V' created by the lines from Bamber Bridge to Preston and Leyland. In 1885 a series of curves at Farrington was authorised by Parliament, the first of which connected the Liverpool line to the LNWR main line. This opened in 1891, allowing trains to run directly into Preston without the need to go via Preston Junction. In anticipation of the opening, a new station had been erected at Lostock Hall directly adjacent to the shed. The second curve was constructed in 1908, and this diverged from the old line just after it crossed the WCML, and then descended to join the 1891 curve at Farrington West. These curves allowed L&YR trains running to Blackpool and Fleetwood easy access into the west side of Preston station, which was essential to avoid conflicting movements with the LNWR's main line traffic.

Closures came apace in the 1960s, though the goods depot at Mill Hill had its service withdrawn as early as 1936. Hoghton was the first passenger station to go in 1960, followed in October 1968 by Preston Junction (renamed Todd Lane in 1952). The line from Cherry Tree to Chorley had been cut back to Feniscowles in 1960, but by the end of 1968 this section had also gone. Finally Lostock Hall went in 1969, a year after the closure of the steam depot — which (like Rose Grove) was one of the last strongholds of steam. The other stations remained, but all served by DMUs and with no goods facilities. The Bamber Bridge-Todd Lane-Preston line closed in May 1972, on completion of the Preston re-signalling programme, causing trains to follow once again the original ELR route via Farrington. Today the rest of the route is still extant, and since 1984 forms part of a trans-Pennine route to Leeds via Todmorden and Bradford. After negotiating the tight curve at Farrington, the WCML is crossed by a flying bridge before the train squeals into Lostock Hall where a station was reopened in 1984. Bamber Bridge is still a minor hive of railway activity, with sidings for the Civil Engineer's Dept, Whittle's Distribution and grain traffic. There then follows some very attractive countryside as the line heads towards Blackburn passing through the now basic stations at Mill Hill and Cherry Tree. On the immediate approach to Blackburn a coal concentration depot occupies the site of the old King Street goods depot, and nearby a distribution depot has its own sidings.

The Blackburn Railway

The Blackburn, Darwen & Bolton Railway was first conceived in 1844, but from the outset it was hoped that this would form part of

a trunk route from Bolton to Settle via the (little) North Western Railway. The BD&BR Act of 1845 authorised the line from Bolton to Blackburn and the first sod was cut on 27 September. The route crossed a high spur from the Pennines between Entwistle and Darwen, and substantial engineering works were required to keep gradients within acceptable limits. While the work on this line was going on, the Blackburn, Clitheroe & North Western Junction Railway Act was passed on 27 July 1846. Work commenced on the extension at Clitheroe in December 1846, but thereafter progressed very slowly. The section from Blackburn to Sough opened on 3 August 1847, but hopes of a speedy progression southwards were marred when four arches on the Tonge Viaduct at Bolton collapsed the same day. The 2,015yd-long tunnel at Sough was also giving problems, but the section through Darwen continued to generate encouraging levels of traffic until the whole route opened the following June.

Unfortunately, the extension beyond Blackburn was still making very little headway due to a variety of reasons - mainly a lack of cash. The bad winter of 1849/50 further delayed progress, as did the partial collapse of Whalley Viaduct. Yet work picked up in the spring, and in June a single line opened to Chatburn (two miles beyond Clitheroe) along with a short branch to Horrocksford. Access to Blackburn was dependent on running powers over a ¾-mile section of the ELR from Daisyfield Junction, but excessive tolls and heavy-handed tactics by the Bury company marred the new line's first week of operation.

The Blackburn Railway had become associated with the L&YR in April 1850, and the larger railway took over the entire operating side of the company from May. As this left the Blackburn Railway without any control over the day to day working of their line, they were very much at the L&YR's mercy. Soon the L&YR began to starve the smaller concern of traffic in order to 'run it down', and thereby absorb it at a very low price. By 1856 enough was enough and, in desperation, the Blackburn Railway began talking about their own direct line into Manchester, followed (in 1857) by a re-emergence of the proposals to extend the line north of Chatburn. Finally, the issue was resolved when the L&YR and ELR put forward a joint take-over bid, and the Blackburn railway was absorbed by its two neighbours on 1 January 1858.

From around 1859 all train services were diverted into the former-ELR station in Blackburn which then required enlargement, a task that was completed in the early 1860s. The traffic that was now originating from north Lancashire and passing through Bolton to Manchester presented severe operating difficulties over the LNWR metals from Salford to Victoria until the L&YR opened its own

Below:
Since December 1985 Bromley Cross, between Bolton and Blackburn, has enjoyed the distinction of being a fringe box in both directions with Preston panel covering the line to the north and Bolton to the south. On 28 June 1988, a pair of Class 142s (Nos 142032 and 142040) form the 15.06 Blackburn-Manchester Victoria.
Paul D. Shannon

Left:
A primary objective of the new Hellifield line was a Manchester-Carlisle/Scotland service, which would give the L&YR a freight route to the far north. To provide suitable clearance for the larger Midland and Pullman stock, tunnels on the Manchester-Blackburn route had to be given greater clearances and at Sough the trackbed had to be lowered by no less than 15in. Prior to the completion of this work, the Midland ran their trains via Bury, Colne and Skipton although a limited service ran via Hellifield from 1882 onwards. The difference in the L&YR and Midland loading gauges can best be illustrated in this picture of a double-headed passenger train at Langho, the leading coach being a Midland clerestory with L&YR stock behind. *B. C. Lane Collection*

Left:
Passenger services over the Blackburn-Hellifield route, except for diversions and specials, were withdrawn on 10 September 1962. Langho station, however, had closed six years earlier on 7 May 1956. Although the northbound platform remains, there is little else to show the residents of the new housing development on 17 June 1992 that there was once a station here. The local authorities are currently investigating the possibility of reintroducing regular passenger services over the line and, if this progresses, a number of new stations, including Langho, will be built. *Gavin Morrison*

Left:
Though it is one of the few L&YR branch lines to survive, the short Horrocksford branch is retained only for freight traffic. It has survived by virtue of the Castle cement works which originates sufficient traffic to quell BR's insatiable appetite for closing small branch lines and is, therefore, a vital link in keeping heavy goods traffic off the narrow roads in the locality. In June 1986 No 31275, in Railfreight livery, heads south past the junction with engineers' train to Blackburn. *Paul D. Shannon*

Above:

In 1956 DMUs were introduced between Bury and Bacup, replacing the 2-4-2 tank engines and offering a service every half-hour (every 15min on Saturdays) from early morning to midnight. The trains were not exactly packed, but they were very well used and several were extended through to Manchester. Ludicrously, the service did not fit into the 'Beeching idyll' and was therefore earmarked for closure. On 30 July 1958 a Metro-Cammell two-car set headed by No M79077 waits in the terminus at Bacup with a noon working for Bury.
T. K. Widd

Above right:

With the closure of both routes into Bacup, this part of East Lancashire became dependent on a totally inadequate road system and it showed. Meanwhile, the railways became walkways, dumping grounds and building sites as the process of decay was accentuated. On the outskirts of Bacup the trackbed is already disappearing beneath a mound of rubble in this 1987 view, even though the fine stone work of the overbridge and culvert bear still bear testimony to the mason's art.
Dave Ibbotson

connection between these points in 1865. This greatly improved the prospects for the long-held ambition of extending north from Chatburn to Long Preston. Yet, when the tender for the extension was finally awarded in 1873, the destination had been changed to Hellifield to connect with the Midland Railway's proposed line from Settle to Carlisle. That route opened in May 1876, but the L&YR only completed their line to Hellifield in the spring of 1879. Even then, because the new junction station was not complete, the 'Lanky' had to be content with a passenger terminus at Gisburn for a further year. The additional traffic that the new route would entail threatened to overwhelm the station at Blackburn, so between 1885-86 a new one was erected — thus allowing the working of all the Scottish trains through the town from 1888 onwards.

The LMS made great use of the ex-L&YR line to Hellifield routeing many principal express workings this way. In addition it also provided a very useful diversionary route for the WCML. Regretfully, the countryside it traversed was too rural and intermediate stations were poorly patronised after World War 2. Oaks was the first to be abandoned in 1950, followed by Langho in 1956 and Newsholme a year later. Then Spring Vale (Sough), Lower Darwen, Daisyfield and Rimmington all went in a spate of 1958 closures. By the end of 1962 only Bromley Cross, Entwistle and Darwen were left between Blackburn and Bolton, whilst the line to Hellifield was totally devoid of local passenger trains (and stations) from September 1962. This left one remaining scheduled passenger working, a Manchester-Glasgow Saturday service, but this was withdrawn in 1964.

Fortunately the Hellifield line's value as a freight and diversionary route ensured its survival, though several questions on its future were raised during the debate about the Settle & Carlisle Railway. Dales Rail has provided a useful service into the Yorkshire Dales and Cumbria via the line, and these

trains call at Clitheroe. In 1990 BR took over this service from the local authority and, whilst it remains well-supported, 1991 saw a reduction in the numbers of trains operated. At the time of writing a number of experimental passenger workings have been operated to the reopened station at Clitheroe, and discussions continue between BR and Lancashire County Council regarding the introduction of a regular service. The proposed hourly service would originate at Preston or Manchester and beyond Blackburn call at Whalley, Langho and Wilpshire, with possible appropriate extensions beyond Clitheroe to Hellifield - thus permitting connection with Settle-Carlisle line services.

From Bolton Junction the now singled line heads south, and then commences the climb which takes it past the site of Hoddlesden Junction. Between 1876 and 30 October 1950 goods trains diverged here for the 2½-mile long branch to Hoddlesden which, despite entreaties by the local populace, was never served by regular passenger trains. The former main line is now singled, but has a passing loop at Darwen before trains begin the climb to Sough. After ploughing through the summit tunnel the long descent to Bolton commences, passing through Entwistle station which is still operational and often used by walkers making for the nearby moorlands. As the line continues to the attractive station at Bromley Cross the carriage window provides picturesque views over the Wayoh and Tumbles reservoirs. The track then becomes double down to Astley Bridge, and the panorama changes from rural to suburban indicating that the train is now rolling down to the new station at Hall i' th' Wood and thus to Bolton.

The Bacup Branch

When the East Lancashire Railway reached Rawtenstall in September 1846, there were already moves afoot to extend the line further up the valley by building a branch line to Bacup. The Act for this was passed in July

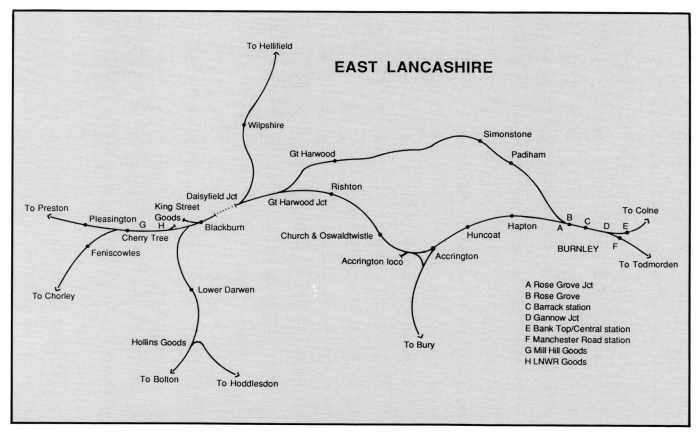

EAST LANCASHIRE

To Hellifield

Wilpshire

Simonstone

Gt Harwood

Padiham

Rishton

Daisyfield Jct

King Street
Goods

Gt Harwood Jct

To Preston

Pleasington   G

Blackburn

To Colne

B

C

D   E

Cherry Tree

Church & Oswaldtwistle

Hapton   A

Feniscowles

Huncoat

BURNLEY   F

Accrington loco

Accrington

To Chorley

To Todmorden

A Rose Grove Jct
B Rose Grove
C Barrack station
D Gannow Jct
E Bank Top/Central station
F Manchester Road station
G Mill Hill Goods
H LNWR Goods

Lower Darwen

Hollins Goods

To Bury

To Bolton

To Hoddlesdon

1846 but work did not begin until early the following year, and then it was only a single line of rails built on a double-track formation. By May financial problems were nibbling away at the project, and it was decided to suspend the work above Newchurch. This line from Rawtenstall to Newchurch opened in March 1848, but the real goal was still Bacup despite the fact that three tunnels (totalling 466yd) were needed to make this extension a reality. Work on the suspended section began again in September 1851, and the single line opened to Bacup 13 months later. Doubling commenced in 1878, and the new 592yd-long Thrutch Tunnel was built to duplicate the full length of the two shorter bores at Newchurch, whilst the one at Bacup was actually widened to accommodate double track. In view of the doubling and in preparation of the opening of the branch line from Rochdale, Bacup station was rebuilt in 1881, and during the following year a new engine shed was provided between the station and Britannia.

The ELR branch to Bacup carried the bulk of the passenger traffic, whilst the quieter

Left:
Early on the morning of 8 July 1950, a 'Compound' 4-4-0 pilots a 'Black Five' through Summerseat station before running round the train W634, which was an excursion from Bury to Blackpool Central. However, in a number of instances, it was found to be more convenient to start these trains north of Bury. Though steam was completely eliminated on BR 18 years later, the residents of the small Pennine village were to again hear the echo of exhaust blasts across the valley after the East Lancashire Railway reopened the line to Ramsbottom.
Oliver F. Carter

85

Above:

Bury Bolton Street station was the original East Lancashire Railway's headquarters. Seen here in c1915, the station has its main buildings constructed on the road overbridge, with the platforms below. The L&YR station buildings were destroyed by fire in the early 1950s, when a more utilitarian structure was built on the site. The 'new' station was to last until 1980 when services were diverted to the new rail/bus interchange in the town.
Author's Collection

Above right:

After closure the station (and the line) passed to the new East Lancashire Railway as the railway's southern terminus.   The 1950s-built station building demonstrates the new owner's title in January 1992.
Author

Rochdale branch suffered the indignity of having its passenger service 'temporarily' suspended during the 'fuel crisis' of 1947, though it was never to be restored. However, when the Bury-Bacup service was earmarked for closure by Dr Beeching the Minister of Transport found the proposals too harsh and reprieved the line as far as Rawtenstall. After the section on to Bacup closed in December 1966, the remaining trains running north from Bury were repeatedly cut back in frequency until they no longer appealed to the travelling public! Having become grossly unprofitable they were then withdrawn in June 1972 after a means of providing an alternative bus service had been found. However, the line remained open for goods traffic due to the establishment of the coal concentration depot at Rawtenstall — a task it continued for a further eight years, by which time the preservationists were ready to move in. In all, the Bacup branch had fared much better than its neighbouring branch from Bury, that to Holcombe Brook — which met an untimely demise despite being a pioneer of electric traction when it lost its passenger service in April 1952 before being closed completely in 1963.

The East Lancashire Railway Preservation Society

In 1968 the East Lancashire Railway Preservation Society was formed with a view to preserving a section of line from Stubbins Junction to Haslingden. However, the membership contained a mixture of people with differing objectives. Some wished to save the line to provide a local passenger service whilst others saw it as means to preserve steam traction which was being phased out on British Railways that August. This conflict of interests did not produce the desired effects, and the ELRPS languished in a state of flux for many years. Yet the society slowly gathered momentum, and by 1972 they were able to start collecting a number of redundant locomotives after Bury Council leased them the old East Lancashire Railway goods shed at Bury. With a peppercorn rental being charged, the impetus was provided and the old goods yard was slowly developed into a transport museum.

Around the same time the Bury-Rawtenstall passenger service was withdrawn, leaving the line used solely for coal traffic from Castleton to Rawtenstall. When this traffic ended in 1980 the local authorities stepped in and prevented the line from being lifted, and this was the fillip the society needed. With assistance from Greater Manchester County Council, Bury Metropolitan Council and Rossendale Borough Council the trackbed and infrastructure were secured. A partnership was then formed to enable the railway to be opened between Bury and Rawtenstall, the participants being: the East Lancashire Railway Preservation Society, whose members provide the voluntary labour force; the East Lancashire Light Railway Co, which leases the railway and is responsible for its day to day running and operation; the East Lancashire Railway Trust, which administers the grant funds for the development of the railway — the trust currently being made up from representatives of Bury MBC, Rossendale BC and directors of the railway company — but shortly to be joined be a representative from Rochdale Metropolitan Council.

The next important step also came in 1980, when the opening of Bury Interchange station meant that Bolton Street station was available for the establishment of the society's headquarters. In the following years enthusiastic volunteers, supported by employees on job creation/training schemes, enabled the line to be reopened from Bolton Street to Ramsbottom on 25 July 1987. At Ramsbottom a new station had to be built on the site of the original ELR station, and this was constructed to a traditional ELR design. The platform was subsequently furnished with a new 'parachute' water tower, this being made up from original L&YR drawings. However, the society were not content to stop there, and on 27 April 1991 the extension to Rawtenstall

was formally opened by the mayors of Bury and Rossendale.

Unfortunately, during August 1991, the connection to the BR network via the electric line at Buckley Wells was lost, when the Crumpsall-Bury section closed in preparation for the line's conversion to Metrolink. Undeterred, the society had already identified an eastern exit, along the old trackbed to Heywood. Though this had seen no regular traffic for over a decade, the line stretched tantalisingly towards the M&L main line at Rochdale. However, between Bury and Heywood, a new bridge would have to be built over the Metrolink line and a new bridge deck laid at Pilsworth. Though Heywood station has been demolished, both platforms remain and after observing the station at Ramsbottom (and the new one now nearing completion at Rawtenstall), one imagines that this should not be a major obstacle. In cooperation with London Carriers Ltd at Heywood, it is hoped that the railway will have an interesting future as a freight operator — and a shunting locomotive has been purchased for the purpose.

Meanwhile, another pressing ambition is for the society to acquire the former electric car sheds at Buckley Wells (the original ELR's locomotive works). This project, which the author has happily been involved with, began at the end of 1991 after BR moved out the last of its equipment from the property and, if realised, will provide the society with the finest workshop premises on any preserved railway in the country today.

Powell-Duffryn — Standard Wagon Co

The Standard Wagon Co has long traditions and an interesting history, and though space does not permit a full account of the company's development it is of specific interest because its presence at Heywood has ensured the survival of the line down to Castleton. Originally owned by the Lancashire & Yorkshire Wagon Co, the works were taken over by Standard Wagon Co of Reddish in the 1960s and a manufacturing and leasing division was established at Heywood. The company's 'Rail-lease' fleet was sold to Procor when they established their base in the United Kingdom, with Standard Wagon gaining the contract to supply them with new wagons. However, when Procor acquired the manufacturing capacity of Charles Roberts Ltd., Standard went back into the lease of wagons but having the advantage of an all new fleet.

Since acquisition by the Powell-Duffryn Group, the company's products have been substantially improved and are now aimed particularly at the European market. Design studies are well advanced for a new generation of railway wagons and wagon bogies, rated at speeds of up to 90 mph (140km/h). High capacity hopper and tank wagons, low-deck height container wagons and self discharging trains are all an important part of the company's marketing strategy. Yet the greatest development seems to be in the field of track friendly bogie systems, with the Gloucester LTF bogies representing a radical new approach to conventional designs by having a long wheelbase with small diameter wheels. This substantially reduces the wheelset mass over traditional designs allowing improved riding characteristics, reduced operating costs and minimising environmental impact. Little of the original works are left today, and access off the Heywood branch was changed when the road was improved and a new automated crossing put in. The old goods yard is now used for wagon storage, but part of the station site has been handed over to the East Lancs Railway.

6

Greater Manchester

The Stalybridge Branch

In discussing the lines which radiated from Manchester, the branch from Miles Platting to Stalybridge is a good place to begin, as this was the third M&L branch to be authorised. The Ashton, Stalybridge & Liverpool Junction Railway was approved in July 1844, but despite the apparently easy terrain, the 6½ miles presented the builders with a number of major obstacles. Two large viaducts were required, the first of which was a timber trestle at Park, the second being a more substantial structure across the Medlock. Next came the bogs of Ashton Moss, which the contractors could only negotiate with extreme difficulty; to cross the Moss, brushwood and clay foundations had to be laid to a depth of five to six feet below the trackbed. Yet, despite all this, the work progressed quickly and the branch opened as far as Ashton-under-Lyne in April 1846, followed by the remaining section to Stalybridge six months later.

The single track terminated at the same point as the Sheffield, Ashton & Manchester's branch to Stalybridge and a joint station was erected. Both companies hoped to use Stalybridge as a springboard for a direct assault on the Pennines at Standedge, but they were beaten to the task by the Huddersfield & Manchester Railway in 1849, and the LNWR trains began using the branch to gain access into Victoria from the late summer onwards. In anticipation of this traffic, the branch was doubled during 1847-48, and this work was fully completed by January 1850. In 1861 the timber trestle at Park was converted to an embankment, but within two decades more severe difficulties were encountered with sub-

sidence below the 10-arch Medlock Viaduct. Accordingly a new viaduct was authorised in 1886, but even this suffered from subsidence and heavy bracing is still evident on the structure today.

Beside the LNWR express trains, the branch enjoyed a steady flow of local traffic, and intermediate stations were provided at Ashton-under-Lyne, Droylsden, Clayton Bridge and Park. At Miles Platting a new junction station was erected to serve both the main line and the branch. A useful extension to the branch was opened in 1848, when a 1 mile 1,561yd-long connecting line opened to the LNWR at Ardwick. A triangular junction at Park led to the Ardwick branch, which provided a convenient route for sending trains to the south of Manchester, and it was used by both freight and passenger trains - a short branch of this line served a goods depot at Beswick. This convenient route is still extant, as is the curve from the Stalybridge branch to Brewery Sidings on the M&L main line.

Though the Stalybridge branch is still in use, it has seen a considerable reduction in passenger trains since all of the trans-Pennine express workings were diverted into Piccadilly in 1989. Droylsden and Clayton Bridge stations closed their doors to passengers in October 1968, but a feasibility study is currently being undertaken with a view to a reopening at Droylsden. Stalybridge has been attractively refurbished in recent years, but at Ashton the island platform has been ravaged by the removal of surplus buildings, though it is well kept. The same can not be said for Park (with its derelict cattle docks nearby) and

Below left:
Most people who have travelled over the Pennines along the Standedge route will fail to appreciate that the 'Premier Line' depended on the L&YR for two substantial sections of their route from Manchester to Leeds. On the western side of the Pennines, this was achieved by the LNWR gaining running powers over the L&YR's Stalybridge branch to Miles Platting and from there into Manchester's Victoria or Exchange stations. One such occasion is captured when extra working C900 is pictured as 'Black 5' 4-6-0 No 45371 heads a nine-coach through Ashton-under-Lyne.
Kenneth Field

Below:
Class 142 No 142096 heads north towards Ashton in June 1992 with a service across the Pennines. The considerable reduction in the area's railway facilities is all too clear, although the stone wall has, in the past quarter century, been repointed.
Gavin Morrison

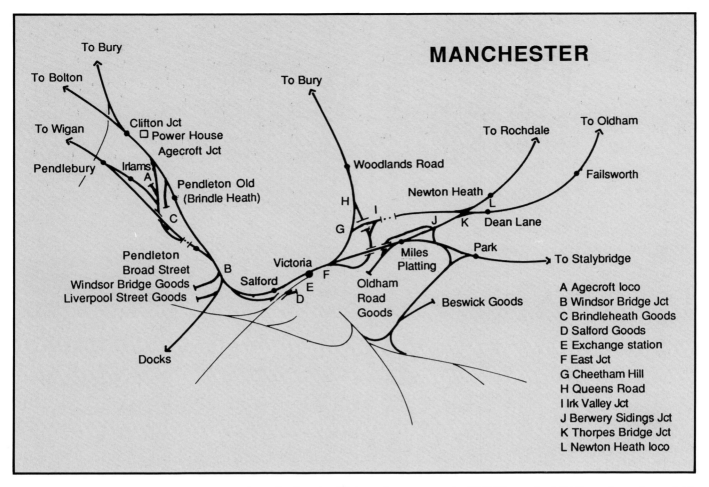

MANCHESTER

To Bury
To Bolton
To Wigan
Clifton Jct
◻ Power House
Agecroft Jct
Pendlebury
Irlams
A
Pendleton Old
(Brindle Heath)
C
Pendleton
Broad Street
Windsor Bridge Goods
Liverpool Street Goods
B
Salford
Victoria
E
F
D
Docks

To Bury
Woodlands Road
H
G
I
Oldham
Road
Goods
Miles
Platting
Beswick Goods

To Rochdale
To Oldham
Newton Heath
L
Failsworth
J
K
Dean Lane
Park
→ To Stalybridge

A Agecroft loco
B Windsor Bridge Jct
C Brindleheath Goods
D Salford Goods
E Exchange station
F East Jct
G Cheetham Hill
H Queens Road
I Irk Valley Jct
J Berwery Sidings Jct
K Thorpes Bridge Jct
L Newton Heath loco

Miles Platting, both of which only see a handful of passengers each day and are being considered for closure. The long term prospects for the branch are uncertain, and if the Standedge line is electrified this might signal its closure, yet parts of it would seem ripe for conversion if the Metrolink system is expanded in the future.

The Oldham Loop

It will be recalled from Chapter 1, that the first line to Oldham diverged from the M&L near Middleton and terminated at Werneth on the west side of the town. The main difficulties of the original branch were its steep incline, and the inconvenient terminal point. The latter issue was resolved in 1847, when two tunnels were bored through a 40ft high ridge of solid rock which lay just beyond Oldham Station. The line was thus extended into a more central but equally inconvenient location at Mumps, after which the original station assumed the more correct title of Werneth. Unfortunately, this still left the incline to contend with, and though rope haulage was probably discontinued by the end of the decade, locomotives still faced the awesome task of battling up a 1 in 27 gradient. The main difficulty lay in the fact that the M&L line was situated at 343ft above sea level, whilst Werneth stood at some 525ft. In 1856

the LNWR reached Oldham from Greenfield, and the L&YR allowed these trains to use Mumps station until an LNWR station was completed nearby.

The next stage of development came with the Oldham, Ashton & Guide Bridge Joint Railway (LNWR/MS&LR), which opened in 1861, giving a through service to Manchester London Road. This new line had a terminus in Clegg Street, the provision of which allowed the closure of the LNWR station at Mumps. The L&YR responded to this challenge by opening a station between Werneth and Mumps, just across the road from Clegg Street, which it pithily called Central. Though it was built to upstage the interlopers, it had a positive benefit for passengers as an interchange between the two stations was quite easily achieved. Likewise a spur for the exchange of freight traffic was built, linking the two lines just north of Clegg Street. The real problem lay with the OA&GBJR's proposals to extend their line to Rochdale and Bacup, so the L&YR had to act quickly to protect its territory.

Goods trains began running to Rochdale in August 1863, with passenger services commencing three months later. On 21 March 1864, the associated branch line to Royton opened. Intermediate stations were provided at Royton Junction, Shaw, New Hey, and

Left:
By way of contrast, today's motive power on the Stalybridge-Manchester Victoria passenger trains tends to be confined to DMU operation following the diversion of express workings into Manchester Piccadilly. On **17 September 1991** Class 142 No 142052, from Newton Heath depot trundles through Ashton station with the **10.23** Wakefield Westgate-Manchester Victoria train.
Author

Centre left:
The Oldham-Rochdale extension had been surveyed by the M&L as early as **1847**, then promptly dropped by the L&YR due to their terrible financial difficulties, but with slight modifications the plan was resubmitted to Parliament in **1859** and duly authorised. The extension also provided the first stage in a route to Royton, an important manufacturing district north of Oldham. In June 1957 '4MT' 2-6-4T No 42647 pulls a Royton-Manchester Victoria train away from Royton Junction station after attaining the 'main line'.
J. Davenport

Left:
The branch from Royton to Royton Junction closed on **18 April 1966** and the impressive array of sidings have all disappeared. Now replaced by Derker, the original Royton Junction station is closed but its weed-strewn platforms remain. In July 1992 Class 142 No 142055 heads north into the station as it makes its way towards Rochdale. The Oldham loop is one of the BR lines that could eventually form part of the expanded Manchester Metrolink project.
Gavin Morrison

Milnrow, but there were none on the branch to Royton. Through services to Manchester began operating on the new line at an early stage, but the real difficulties lay in the size of trains which could manage Werneth Incline. Any improvement to the original route would have been exceptionally difficult so, with the exception of a branch line to Chadderton which opened in August 1914, no major development took place west of Werneth station. The future for the Oldham service was principally centred on a new route to the town from Thorpes Bridge via Hollinwood. This had been authorised in 1847, but other considerations prevented its becoming a reality until 1880. Stations were then provided at Dean Lane, Failsworth and Hollinwood with the two lines reuniting just to the west of Werneth station.

After the inauguration of the Bury electric service in 1916, it had been intended to extend the system to Oldham, but this failed to materialise due to wartime restrictions and a serious lack of resources. Therefore steam remained on all the lines around Oldham, even though the electric sets would have made easy work of the steep lines. This remained the basic position until the intro-

duction of DMUs in 1958, but the Cravens sets used on the service almost shook themselves to bits up Werneth Incline and frequently struggled up the 1 in 50 gradient via Hollinwood. Several of the DMUs developed pyrotechnical tendencies, and fires aboard these units caused serious concern and a hasty scramble to find replacement stock – all factors which had an adverse effect on public confidence and loadings suffered as a result! Passenger services were withdrawn from between Middleton and Werneth in 1960, and the last 'passenger' train was a special drawn by two ex-L&YR locos on 17 September that year; this was followed by complete closure just 28 months later. Beeching saw the lines around Oldham as a prime candidate for 'modification', and the area would have been ravaged if all his suggestions had been implemented. Objections to closure prevented a complete withdrawal, but services were savagely pruned and the Royton branch closed on 16 April 1966 along with Central station, though the passenger service to Rochdale escaped by the skin of its teeth.

Leaving Thorpes Bridge Junction the line passes through the basic station at Dean Lane, after which the rail-served Waste Dis-

Below right:
Wigan was very much an important centre for both the L&YR and the LNWR. Both companies' stations are still extant and are separated only by a couple of hundred yards and a few feet in elevation. Access to the L&YR station was from a street level booking hall, pictured here with Wigan Corporation Tramway's No 41 passing by.
B. C. Lane Collection

Below right:
From the mid-1960s repeated threats faced the Liverpool-Rochdale line, and goods services were removed from intermediate stations between 1961 and 1964 while passenger trains went over to DMU operation from 1965 onwards. The valuable Wigan-avoiding line, which opened between Pemberton and Hindley in 1889, was finally closed to all traffic in 1969. Passengers who travel west of Wigan still have the benefit of all the intermediate stations, but most are just basic halts. On a misty Saturday morning, 17 August 1991, two Class 150 DMUs have just connected up to form an early morning working to Southport with No 150145 in the rear having come from Manchester ECS.
Martin Eltham

92

Above:
Pictured on Easter Saturday, 16 April 1960, 'Black 5' No 44782 prepares to depart from Wigan (Wallgate) with the 1.7pm Manchester Victoria-Southport service. In the background the West Coast main line passes overhead; immediately to the west of the bridge, the L&YR route split with the line to Liverpool, via Kirkby, diverging southwards.
T. Lewis

Left:
Inevitably the past 30 years have seen considerable rationalisation at Wigan (Wallgate) with the curtailment of the bay platform and the conversion of the southernmost platforms to form the ubiquitous car park. The twin water columns have also disappeared, but the station retains its importance as a junction for the two lines to Southport and Kirkby. The more positive aspect of the modern railway scene is visible on the now electrified West Coast main line, with an InterCity-liveried express powering north.
Author

posal Plant is seen adjacent to the down line. Thereafter the line passes through uninspiring countryside, with two rather drab and basic stations at Failsworth and Hollinwood. In the case of the latter station, this will probably be completely rebuilt around 1993-94, when a new bridge for the Manchester Ring Road will affect the present site. The depressing sight of breeze-block platforms and porta-cabin shelters at Oldham Werneth contrast vividly with the buildings erected when this was the town's original station. In complete contrast, Mumps station is a pleasant mixture of old and new; its original L&YR canopies have been retained and tastefully painted, but the station has been completely modernised during 1991 providing the most up to date facilities. In 1987 a new station was erected at Derker, thus allowing the closure of the station at Royton Junction which had been in an inconvenient location since the closure of the branch line.

After the old junction, the line heads into more pleasant countryside to arrive at Shaw and Crompton. Up to 1897 this station was simply called Shaw, a name to which it

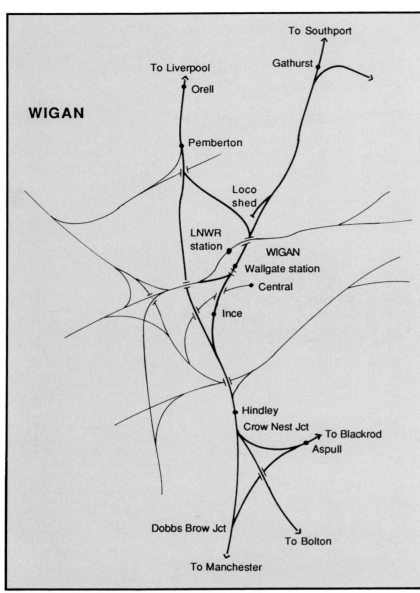

WIGAN

To Southport
Gathurst
To Liverpool
Orell
Pemberton
Loco shed
LNWR station
WIGAN
Wallgate station
Central
Ince
Hindley
Crow Nest Jct
To Blackrod
Aspull
Dobbs Brow Jct
To Bolton
To Manchester

reverted in 1974. However, due to local requests the dual name has now been revived and the PTE are considering the provision of a manned booking office. North of Shaw the former double track section has been reduced to a single track up to the junction with the main line just north of Rochdale. New Hey's station is rather basic, but the old L&YR cotton warehouse (now used for road-haulage purposes) has its original function clearly proclaimed in large white lettering. At Milnrow only the Up platform is in use, its timber deck contrasting with the disused L&YR stone platform on the opposite side. Just before the branch joins the main line north of Rochdale, a large notice can be seen advising drivers of goods trains to stop 'and pin down wagon brakes — regrettably this sign is completely superfluous, as the only freight trains to use the branch are those between Thorpes Bridge Junction and the waste terminal at Dean Lane.

If the Oldham-Rochdale phase of the Metrolink scheme goes ahead, an alternative to converting the existing route through Oldham would be the construction of a heavily engineered section between Werneth and Mumps serving the town centre. Needless to say, such a provision would be very expensive to construct! A further option would be the extension of the light railway services right into the centre of Rochdale.

Wigan

Though Wigan was at the centre of a massive complex of railway lines, much of the town's rail network was developed by the LNWR, having evolved from the North Union Railway. The L&YR found its way into Wigan via the Liverpool & Bury Railway, a scheme devised to break the L&M's monopoly of traffic to the Mersey ports. The Manchester, Bolton & Bury Railway had first

proposed a branch to Wigan in 1834, but even though this would have reduced the rail distance between the two towns by as much as 10 miles it failed to come to fruition. In 1844 a group of prominent businessmen from central Lancashire got together to promote a line from Wigan to Bolton, the idea was warmly received and by 1845 it had been decided to extend the line to Liverpool in the west and Bury in the east. To protect the projected line from the machinations of L&M, the directors decided to join forces with the M&L who were keen to extend from Heywood to Bury. Around the same time, the Manchester & Southport Railway began promoting a direct line to the developing coastal resort via Wigan and Burscough. As the M&L were involved with both lines, it was decided that they should share a joint three-mile section of track through Wigan.

Work on the L&B began early in 1846 but it was not an easy route to construct, and on

Facing page, bottom:
The L&YR's development round Wigan was very slow, and the section to Burscough was not doubled until 1861-62 while the direct, or 'Atherton' line from Wigan to Manchester, was not built until the late 1880s. The same was not true on the line to Bolton, for at a very early stage the line was provided with quite extensive facilities and substantial station buildings were erected at places like Westhoughton. This view is the oldest L&YR picture in the book, dating from the 1860s, and shows a Hawkshaw 2-2-2 with a motley assortment of rather basic four-wheel coaches at Westhoughton.
B. C. Lane Collection

Left:
West of Wigan local goods traffic went into sharp decline after 1958, and the various goods yards closed between 1962 and 1965 on both the Liverpool and Southport lines. However, Gathurst, on the Southport line, maintained a private delivery siding for the munitions depot there. Though this traffic has now ceased, freight trains still use this line to the Waste Disposal Terminal at Appley Bridge. On 22 May 1991 No 47440 leaves Appley Bridge with 6J77 the 17.45 Brindle Heath/Dean Lane empties.
Paul D. Shannon

both approaches to Wigan substantial timber viaducts had to be built, with their foundations resting on piles sunk deep into the ground. Though the railway took a circuitous route to the north, it proved to be an immediate success when it opened in November 1848. On the section of line through Wigan, intermediate stations were provided at Orrell, Pemberton, Wigan, Hindley, Westhoughton and Chew Moor. This latter station closed sometime in the early 1850s, about the time that a new station was provided at Lostock Junction — another addition was the station at Ince which opened around 10 years later.

The Act for the Manchester & Southport Railway was authorised in April 1847, but the M&L manifested little enthusiasm about commencing the project. Meanwhile, the Liverpool, Ormskirk & Preston Railway's scheme for a line from Ormskirk to Southport was rejected, but only after the M&S Act had promised to provide a connection with the LO&P at Burscough. Unfortunately, a delay in starting the M&S line led to a period of some acrimony, and when work finally began it was just limited to the Wigan section. Once this was completed the L&YR seemed prepared to let matters rest. However, a writ of mandamus was issued against the company in August 1852 compelling them to start work at once. The L&YR, beset with financial difficulties, grudgingly issued the contracts - but only for a single track line.

By this time the LO&P had become part of the East Lancashire Railway and, still desiring access to Southport, they proposed that the line west of Burscough be built as a joint project. The L&YR, keen to ease its financial burdens, agreed and by early 1855 the line was ready for opening. However, the Board of Trade was not convinced that a single track from Burscough to Southport was adequate for the traffic it would carry and ordered it to be doubled. The earthworks must have already been built for double track, because a second line of rails was quickly laid, and sanction to open was granted on 4 April. Intermediate stations were opened at Gathurst, Appley Bridge, Newburgh (later Parbold), Burscough Bridge, New Lane, Bescar Lane and the line terminated at Chapel Street in Southport. In the 1870s additional stations were provided at Hoscar and Blowick (renamed Cop End in 1871).

Both of the lines through Wigan enjoyed a considerable level of traffic throughout their L&YR ownership, with the L&B route providing an alternate but fiercely competitive service with the LNWR line, though after 1905 departure times on the two lines were arranged to complement each other giving passengers a more convenient service between Liverpool and Manchester. The Southport line continued to enjoy its heavy seasonal traffic, as well as a moderate number of local passengers during the winter months. At Burscough the south curve permitted a Southport-Ormskirk service until 5 March 1962, but after that saw little use until it was lifted at the end of the 1964 summer season; the north curve was retained only for a further year, despite carrying a large number of holiday trains from the north and east.

Wigan Wallgate has enjoyed several refurbishments in recent years, and the single track bay at the west end has been retained. An interesting feature is the way connections are offered at Wallgate, when up to four DMUs may draw into the platform one behind the other. The station is very well used today and its facilities at platform level comprise a basic booking office, staff area, waiting room and badly vandalised chocolate machines. At street level a booking office, ticket collector's cabin and bookstall are to be found. East of Wigan, Ince has been reduced to just the central platform, connected to the road by a cut-back footbridge. Hindley has only two of its four platforms still in use, and the old westbound trackbed has been turned into a garden decorated with several items of railwayana. Its buildings are now semi-derelict and it is due to be destaffed in the near future, yet it has fared better than Westhoughton which has just a basic platform.

Lostock Junction station, once boasting four platforms with extensive sidings nearby has been swept away following closure in 1966. On 16 May 1988 two timber-built platforms were opened on the line to Chorley and Preston, but trains on the Wigan line have no facilities for stopping there. The reopening of the station was attended by celebrations reminiscent of railway openings in the last century, and the station is so well used that its car park is regularly over subscribed.

The Atherton Line

To the west of Manchester there was a rich area ripe for suburban and industrial traffic, but this had already been exploited by the direct LNWR route to Liverpool. After the Manchester & Southport scheme was abbreviated, the L&YR seemed content with the lengthy journey via Bolton, but eventually resolved this difficulty by opening the direct line to Wigan in October 1888. This left the Bolton line at Windsor Bridge and joined the Liverpool-Bury line at Crow's Nest. A station was erected at Broad Street to give the suburb of Pendleton its second L&YR station, whilst the rest of the line was served by intermediate stations at Pendlebury, Swinton, Moorside & Wardley, Walkden, Atherton and Daisy Hill. A series of spacious twin island stations were provided, most of which were served by street-level booking halls. In June 1889 a spur was turned off at Dobbs Brow, to make a junction with the Hindley-Blackrod branch at Aspull.

ERTON CTL, L&Y.

A slow process of decline began in 1956 when the goods service was withdrawn from Moorside & Wardley; this was followed by the closure of Pendlebury station on 3 October 1960. The remaining stations all stayed open for passenger traffic, but had their goods facilities withdrawn between 1962 and 1964 prior to the line being reduced to double track in 1966. Over the years several proposals have been made for the closure of this line and, though it still carries local trains, the Liverpool expresses passing over the water troughs at Walkden are things of the past. The provision of Salford Crescent means that Pendleton is no longer vital for local residents, and it may face closure in the future. Meanwhile the spur to the Bolton line at Agecroft has now been removed, and the eight-road shed on this line closed on 22 October 1966. The loop line from Brindle Heath to Pendlebury is also just a memory, and the intermediate station at Irlams-o'th'-Height (adjacent to Agecroft shed) closed to passengers in 1956 and completely 10 years later. Atherton's once extensive goods yard has also vanished, and though the BR-pattern signal box is still operational it is some distance back from the track and almost buried in a forest of weeds and shrubs. In May 1987 a new station was erected at Hag Fold (between Atherton and Daisy Hill) to serve a large housing estate, and a further basic halt may be provided at Dobbs Brow Junction in the future.

BOLTON AND BURY

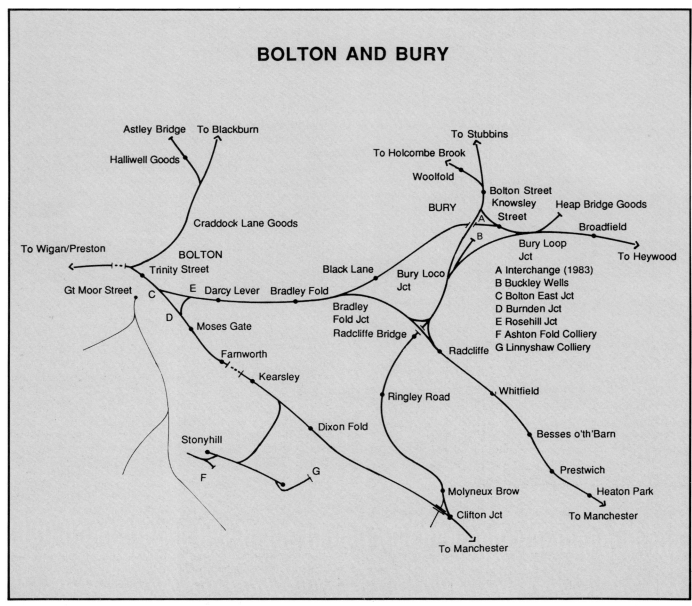

Astley Bridge   To Blackburn

Halliwell Goods

To Stubbins

To Holcombe Brook

Woolfold

Bolton Street
Knowsley
BURY   Street   Heap Bridge Goods

Craddock Lane Goods   Broadfield

To Wigan/Preston   A   Bury Loop
                                                         B   Jct   To Heywood
BOLTON   Black Lane   Bury Loco
Trinity Street   Jct   A Interchange (1983)
                                                              B Buckley Wells
Gt Moor Street   C   C Bolton East Jct
              E Darcy Lever Bradley Fold   D Burnden Jct
         D   Bradley   E Rosehill Jct
              Moses Gate   Fold Jct   F Ashton Fold Colliery
                                   Radcliffe Bridge   G Linnyshaw Colliery
              Farnworth   Radcliffe

              Kearsley   Whitfield

                                Ringley Road

                         Dixon Fold   Besses o'th'Barn

    Stonyhill   Prestwich

    F   G   Heaton Park
                                   Molyneux Brow   To Manchester
                                   Clifton Jct

                              To Manchester

Bolton

Though the Manchester & Bolton Railway opened only on 29 May 1838, almost 10 years later than the B&L (LNWR) line, it was to be of far greater benefit to the rapidly developing town. It was also the first stage in the route to the north, for during the construction period an extension northwards to Preston was actively being pursued. Consequently the opening of the Bolton & Preston Railway followed hot on the heels of the B&L, with the line from Bolton to Rawlinson Bridge opening on 4 February 1839. Chorley became the northern terminus on 22 December 1841 and, after some intense bargaining about the junction with the North Union Railway at Euxton, the railway opened through to Preston in October 1843.

The line to Preston was just two years old when the next major project, the Blackburn, Darwen & Bolton Railway, commenced in September 1845. When this line opened

throughout in 1848, it almost completed Bolton's rail network. There was just one major line left to build — an east-west link: the Liverpool & Bury Railway mentioned in the last section. In the same period, an interesting series of amalgamations took place with the B&P merging with the North Union Railway in 1842, but just two years later the NUR was jointly leased by the Grand Junction and M&L railways. Two years later, the Liverpool & Bury and Manchester & Bolton were both amalgamated into the M&L, and in turn this led to the M&L changing its name to the Lancashire & Yorkshire Railway in 1847.

A number of branch lines were constructed in the area during the 1860s and 70s, the first to be proposed being the cross country route from Hindley to Blackrod and Horwich. This was followed by the construction of the 1 mile 184yd-long Astley Bridge branch, which opened off the Blackburn line in October

98

1877 at a cost of £60,000. However, its investment value was short lived, at least in passenger carrying terms for this service ceased completely just 102 weeks later and thereafter the branch remained solely the domain of freight traffic. In February 1878 the Kearsley and Stony Hill branches opened over Linnyshaw Moss, leaving the M&B line near Kearsley station. The last major development was the construction of a spur from Bradley Fold to Radcliffe in 1879, as part of the new route from Bury to Manchester but which had the added advantage of allowing trains from Bolton to run via the Cheetham Hill route and into the east side of Victoria. Meanwhile, to the north of Bolton the joint operation of the NUR lines continued until 1888-89, when the section from Lostock to Euxton Junction became the sole property of the L&YR.

As will be appreciated, Bolton rapidly became the hub of a substantial railway network, with the L&YR enjoying the bulk of the district's traffic. An enlargement of Trinity Street station was essential as early as 1848, followed by further major alterations in the late 1870s. However, it was the opening of the line to Hellifield, and with it the promise of through traffic over the Settle & Carlisle line, that forced the most drastic changes. Work costing over a quarter of a million pounds started in the summer of 1899 and was not completed until 1903, when 'a magnificent new station' came fully into use. A major change in local services was noted in 1918, after the Bury-Manchester direct line had gone over to electric operation, and the Bolton-Radcliffe-Manchester passenger trains were cut back to Radcliffe Central. From then onwards this working became the haunt of one of the L&YR railmotors, which was also able to serve an intermediate station at Ainsworth Road.

Services remained fairly constant and well-patronised throughout the LMS era, but the ex-LNWR terminus at Great Moor Street

Below left:
It is worth noting that in 1992 the oldest constituent part of the L&YR, the Manchester, Bolton & Bury Canal Co, will celebrate its 200th anniversary having been formed in 1792. The canal opened in 1805, but after the Bolton & Leigh Railway opened in 1831 it seriously affected the canal's business and, in turn, it was proposed to convert the canal into a railway offering a direct route to Manchester. In the end the Manchester & Bolton Railway was built alongside the canal and it opened to Salford on 29 May 1838. Bolton is still a principal centre for rail traffic, and a huge volume of business from a locally based mail-order company has done much to ensure the continued survival of parcel traffic. On 19 July 1990 Nos 31530 and 47543 get ready to leave the parcels platform at Trinity Street with the 16.25 to St Pancras.
Paul D. Shannon

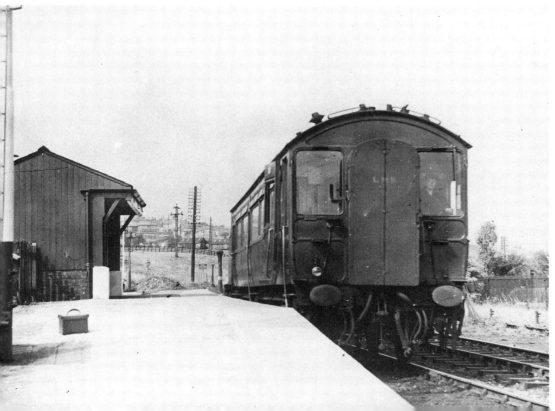

Left:
Rather appropriately, the last remaining haunt of the Horwich-built Hughes railmotors was on the branch from Blackrod to Horwich. Of these, No 10617 was the last survivor and it found gainful employment shuttling back and forth along the line, carrying both local people and employees of the railway works. On 22 April 1947 No 10617, driving trailer first, prepares to set out from Blackrod — a rather pleasant picture, for although these trains spent half their lives travelling in this direction, most published photographs tend to illustrate the locomotive end.
W. Lees courtesy B. C. Lane

Right:
Another location north of
Bolton which has seen major
changes is Lostock Junction.
With the closure of the
station in 1966 and
subsequent simplification of
the track layout the scene
has now changed radically
since steam days. On
12 February 1989 two
Class 20s, Nos 20069 and
20043, pull away from the
junction after running round
the diverted 13.30 Preston-
London Euston service, while
No 47457 pushes at the rear.
Today both the box and
signals are now gone, and
Class 20 locomotives are
rapidly declining in numbers.
Paul D. Shannon

Centre right:
The town of Horwich owed
almost everything to the
railway, and the L&YR went
on to support the
development of all the civic
amenities. The most notable
building being the superb
Mechanics' Institute of 1888,
which became so well used
that it almost doubled in size
within five years. The town's
station was busy at peak
times and when shifts
changed at the works, but it
was often lightly used at
other times. As a
consequence it was ideal for
railmotor operation and in
June 1925 No 10612 waits at
Horwich with a set of
Chorley coaches alongside. In
the far background a large
notice requests passengers to
'Please have your Tickets
and Contracts ready'.
Oliver F. Carter Collection

Below right:
The station at Chorley is
again another curious
mixture of old and new, with
a modern booking hall,
functional platforms and a
timber signalbox operating
the gated level crossing at
the south end. On a wet
20 October 1991 No 150140
passes through the station on
a Manchester-Blackpool
North train. Regrettably the
station's once important
junction status has long since
been removed and today it is
little more than an
intermediate stop on the
route from Bolton to Preston.
Martin Eltham

Left:
In 1918 the 1,200V dc third-rail Bury electric system was extended down the Holcombe Brook line (opened 1881), thereby replacing the experimental Dick-Kerr 3,500V dc overhead system which had been installed along the three-mile branch and between Tottington Junction and Bolton Street in 1913. The branch's 1,200V dc system remained in operation throughout the LMS era, and the first signs of any real alteration was in March 1951 when the electric service between Bury and Holcombe Brook was 'suspended' until further notice due to 'equipment renewal'. Just 14 months later the replacement steam-hauled service was withdrawn, leaving the branch to goods traffic until it was cut back to Tottington in 1960 followed by complete closure in 1963. Here a three-car electric set is seen at the terminus between trips with the conductor/guard resting on a platform seat.
Real Photographs/Ian Allan Library

Left:
The section of the Manchester-Bury third-rail line from Victoria to Crumpsall closed with the 23.30 working on 6 July 1991, and the service to Bury was worked in isolation up to 16 August 1991 when it was also withdrawn and replaced by a temporary bus link. The new Metrolink line is designed to provide a through service from Bury to Deansgate, with the extensions to Altrincham. On the last day of the BR service a persistent drizzle and mist led to poor light conditions, spoiling the opportunity for good photography — out of this mist a graffiti-covered EMU pulls into the station as an early dusk approaches.
Martin Eltham

closed to regular passenger traffic in 1952. However, the exceptional flow of summer specials ensured that it was retained to relieve the pressure on Trinity Street until 1959. In 1963 the Astley Bridge branch was cut back to Halliwell goods yard, where a nearby power station ensured its survival until 3 August 1981. It is worthy of note that, prior to the final closure of this power station, part of the plant was 'taken over' for the reconstruction of Bolton Corporation Tramways car No 66.

The gradual reduction in traffic in the postwar era led to the withdrawal of the passenger trains to Radcliffe in September 1953, followed by the complete closure of the line from Bradley Fold Junction to Radcliffe Central and the west-facing spur from Radcliffe North Junction in October 1964. However, the Radcliffe power station supplying current

for the electrified route was situated adjacent to this spur, and one length of track was left in position as the negative return. Rusted and apparently out of use the metal seemed a prime target for thieves searching for 'scrap'. However, they got rather more than they bargained for — the trains certainly came to an abrupt halt! Had the Picc-Vic scheme gone ahead the Bradley Fold — Radcliffe section would have been reopened, but this of course never came to fruition.

The bulk of Bolton's passenger routes are still open today, but the significant casualty is the link to Bury which was lost in October 1970. The line to Preston still has stations at Lostock, Blackrod, Adlington, and Chorley, but they are all pretty bleak and basic. Euxton is the only casualty, and this closed as long ago as April 1917 at the height of World War 1 staff shortages. On the now singled line to Blackburn, a relatively decent service has been maintained and a new station provided at Hall i' th' Wood just north of Bolton. South of the town the station at Moses Gate lost its goods facilities a quarter of a century ago, but it still handles a modest level of passenger traffic. The twin tunnels at Farnworth follow the station, with their unequal bores being a legacy of the alterations needed to permit through running of the Midland's Pullman cars after the line to Hellifield opened a new route to Scotland in 1880. Kearsley and Clifton also maintain their stations, but the lines which diverged from those points have now been removed.

It is perhaps fitting to conclude with a word on the recent modernisation of Trinity Street, Bolton's only surviving station. In 1987 the L&YR station was modernised at street level to provide a modern bus/rail interchange facility, involving the removal of the gaunt brick building which had previously occupied the site. Today Bolton is an interesting mixture of old and new, a modern upper concourse with lifts (that actually work) taking passengers down to the three platforms that remain in use. Many of the platform buildings have been refurbished though, thankfully, several of the etched glass window panes denoting the original function of the rooms have been retained. Unfortunately, Bolton West signalbox, built in 1921 as one of the first power signal boxes in the country, was swept away as the station came under the control of the Piccadilly Signalling Centre.

Horwich

For over a century Horwich was associated with the railway manufacturing industry, an association which began with the building of the L&YR's engine works that were commenced in 1884-85. Many people view Horwich's development as being solely due to these works, yet in the 1850s it was already a village of around 3,000 inhabitants most of whom were employed in the cotton and bleaching industries. The first stage of rail development came with the line from Hindley to Horwich Road (Blackrod) that opened in the autumn of 1866. The branch into the village itself came slightly later, resulting in a change of name for the main line station which then became Horwich & Blackrod Junction. By 1888 the junction was simply known as Blackrod, as the growing town of Horwich became clearly defined.

The works eventually opened in 1887, occupying part of a 360-acre greenfield site bought for the bargain price of £36,000. The establishment of the works was due to a desire to relocate the L&YR's manufacturing capacity outside Manchester, where the company's cramped workshops were unable to expand successfully to meet the changing needs of the engineering industry. It was almost an entirely self-contained works, with extensive facilities for boiler-making and foundry-work in addition to the general machining, erecting and repair work which was to be carried on. Furthermore the works manufactured a whole variety of railway-related equipment varying from signalling and track parts, and less obvious items like artificial limbs and bed springs. The initial business of the works was related to much needed repair work that had been deferred during the final months at Miles Platting. However the first new locomotive (2-4-2T No 1008 – now preserved) rolled out of the works in January 1889. The works went on to produce another 1,829 main line steam locomotives, five narrow gauge locos, and 169 diesel shunters. During this time it was to produce some notable engineers, including Alliot Verdon-Roe, Fowler, Gresley, Hughes and Maunsell. During World War 1 the works became an important manufacturer of munitions, whilst the cottage hospital was used for the treatment of wounded servicemen. After the Grouping Horwich continued to play an important role in the LMS's locomotive manufacturing capacity, and perhaps the principal type of engine associated with the works during this era was the Class 5MT 2-6-0 — better known to most enthusiasts as the Horwich Crabs. Though it should be said that not all of them were constructed at Horwich, the first of the class (LMS No 13000) was, and by good fortune it too has survived into preservation.

A variety of locomotives were produced through the LMS era, and after the war came the BR Standards, but by then the writing was on the wall. The last steam locomotive, BR Class 2 2-6-0 No 76099, was completed in the autumn of 1957. Thereafter the works concentrated on building 350hp diesel-mechanical shunters, before going over to wagon repairs in 1963. By then around 50,000 engines had passed through the shops for repair. With the decline at the works, the branch line to the town also suffered as passenger services were withdrawn in September 1965 and the goods depot closed the following April. In 1967 the Bolton-facing junction of the Horwich fork closed, and all works traffic used the Chorley-facing arm. Though Horwich Works remained open, a gradual process of closure was implemented. Its later work was quite diversified but the nearest it came to loco-building was maintenance on EMUs. Sadly the plant has now ceased rail operations and Horwich has become a railway town without a railway.

The Bury Line

Though the town of Bury lies within Greater Manchester, its rail development is more correctly associated with East Lancashire discussed in the previous chapter. In 1844 the Manchester, Bury & Rossendale Railway was authorised to build a line from

Clifton Junction on the M&B line to Bury, in preference to the M&L's plans to extend its line from Heywood. The Bury line was eventually extended to run through to Accrington, and a double track was built as far as Stubbins Junction, with single track extensions initially being provided to Bacup and Accrington.

By the time the Bury line opened on 28 September 1846, it had changed its name to the East Lancashire Railway, whilst the B&M had become part of the L&YR. The ELR's access to Manchester was a matter of some contention between the two companies, and an all time low in this relationship was experienced in 1849. The story of the head-on conflict at Clifton Junction is legendary in the annals of railway history and, even though the L&YR backed down, the ELR remained very dissatisfied with the arrangements. Consequently, all the ELR trains terminated at Salford and the company began promoting its own line into the city. The matter was eventually resolved in 1854, when the L&YR directors transferred the line from Clifton Junction into joint ownership. This marked a period of better relationships, and soon the two railways were combining to starve the Bolton, Blackburn, Clitheroe & West Yorkshire Railway of business by diverting Blackburn traffic via Bury and Accrington.

As a consequence the Blackburn Railway decided to promote its own route into Manchester via Radcliffe and Cheetham Hill. Though this scheme was defeated, the proposed railway would have served the same hinterland as that which was traversed by the L&YR's direct line from Radcliffe North Junction. When it opened in September 1879, intermediate stations were situated at White-field, Prestwich, Heaton Park and Crumpsall, with additional stops being provided at Woodlands Road (1913), Besses-o'th'-Barn (1933), and Bowker Vale (1938). A junction was made at Cheetham Hill with the new Victoria East-Thorpes Bridge connecting line bringing trains into a temporary platform at Ducie Street. In 1895 powers were sought to build a line to take the Bury trains into the suburban side of Victoria station by means of a new junction at Queens Road and a tunnel below the Miles Platting Incline at Collyhurst, with a reverse direction spur from Irk Valley to Smedley Viaduct on the connecting line. This viaduct was the scene of a fearful accident claiming 19 lives in 1962, after an up electric train was struck a glancing blow by a Stanier 2-6-4T and plunged into the River Irk below.

The other major development to affect Bury was the cross-country line from Liverpool to Rochdale, which has already been discussed in the sections detailing Wigan and Bolton. The L&B reached Bury from Bolton in November 1848, some six months after the line from Castleton to Heywood had been extended into the town. The two lines made an end-on junction at Knowsley Street, thus allowing through services to begin. Not only did this provide a useful passenger route from Rochdale to Liverpool, but it also allowed freight trains from Yorkshire to reach the Mersey Ports avoiding Manchester. In 1894 the Bury Loop was constructed to provide a cut-off from the Liverpool line just east of Knowsley Street, joining the Manchester line near the loco shed. This was part of the L&YR's scheme for serving the Manchester Ship Canal at Salford, and allowed trains from Yorkshire access to the Docks Branch via Clifton Junction - obviating the need for a reversal at Manchester. Though the docks branch from Windsor Bridge opened in a relatively short period, the parallel connection from Ordsall Lane was not completed until 1988, when on a different alignment it became the Windsor Link.

The railways around Bury have a fascinating history, and regrettably it is too complex to detail in the short space we have available, so we must concentrate on the major developments. The most important of these was the L&YR's decision to electrify the suburban route to Manchester via Radcliffe and Cheetham Hill. Following their experiments with electric traction north of Liverpool, the company decided to adopt a unique 1,200V dc third-rail system between Victoria and Bury Bolton Street. These electric trains began running in April 1916 and, though not all the vehicles were to enter service straight away, it did allow the release of a number of steam engines which were desperately needed because of the wartime locomotive shortages. These changes saw the establishment of regular electric trains between Bolton Street and Victoria, whilst steam trains to north Lancashire would follow the original ELR line from Clifton Junction to Accrington. The trains were usually of a five-car formation on the Manchester workings, whilst two-car sets sufficed for the Holcombe Brook branch — in appearance these handsome all-metal vehicles were not dissimilar to the gangway ended Class 150/2 'Sprinters' introduced seven decades later.

In 1952 the upper concourse of Bolton Street had to be rebuilt with a new booking office following a severe fire which damaged the original ELR buildings. Beginning in 1956 most of the non-electric local services were converted to DMU operation and three years later the life-expired L&YR electric sets were replaced by new BR EMUs (TOPS Class 504) built at the ex-LNWR carriage works at Wolverton. Beeching saw no future for the area's rail network, and his infamous axe was wielded with savage ferocity on 3 December 1966 with the simultaneous closure of the sections of line from Bury to Clifton Junction, Stubbins Junction-Accrington, and Rawtenstall-Bacup.

The following year the Bury Loop was taken out of service after a fire destroyed one of the signalboxes. In October 1970 the Bolton-Rochdale service ceased, and Knowsley Street station was closed. Passenger trains continued from Bolton Street to Rawtenstall until June 1972, after which the only traffic to progress north of Bury were the coal trains which came in through Heywood but this line was closed in December 1980. A further change came in 1980 when the town's third station opened on 17 March, allowing the transfer of trains from Bolton Street to an 'Interchange' station adjacent to the main shopping precinct. This involved a new section of line following the track of the old Bury Loop before cutting across the remains of Knowsley Street station.

Sadly the trains on the Bury service attracted considerable levels of vandalism, and soon became very unpleasant adverts for rail travel in spite of vigorous efforts by the authorities to address the situation. The graffiti covered Class 504 EMUs continued to operate into the new interchange until the summer of 1991, when the service was withdrawn in stages to allow the construction of the Metrolink system. The section from Victoria to Crumpsall closed on 6 July 1991, with the section from Crumpsall to Bury being worked in isolation until 16 August, when it too was withdrawn and replaced by a network of temporary buses.

Metrolink

Manchester's rail network has long suffered from the legacies of its independent origins, with all the various pre-Grouping rail terminals being totally unsuited to unification. Between 1900 and the mid-1920s various schemes were promoted for a circular underground railway to connect the principal stations. By the late 1920s this had changed to a two line underground system, providing north-south and east-west lines with an interchange at Albert Square. But every initiative to provide a cross-city rail service for Manchester and its environs failed for one reason or another, with the demise of the Picc-Vic scheme (which would have brought passengers right into the heart of the city) being a particularly unfortunate casualty.

Whilst the Windsor Link proposals did join the north and south rail networks, such an arrangement failed to penetrate the city. Moreover it put considerable investment into that section of route from Bolton to Stockport, but it did nothing for the remaining lines: these consisted of no less than three electric systems, 25kV ac overhead, 1,500V dc overhead (the remaining parts of the Woodhead electrification scheme) and the unique 1,200V dc third-rail line to Bury. All the other routes were operated by 'Modernisation Plan' era DMUs, which were rapidly reaching a considerable age by the end of the 1970s. In fact the whole of the rolling stock fleet was nearing the point where it would have to be replaced within the coming decade; it was almost a question of redevelop or close!

Thus the idea of light rail germinated in the Greater Manchester PTE's Planning Department long before it showed its head publicly. Throughout 1981 three officers, Tony Young, David Tibke and John Hart, began an evaluation of all the rail routes through their area both operational and closed. They weighed possible routeings, considered segregation from BR involving parallel single tracks, new alignments, flying junctions and so forth — all in addition to their ordinary duties. By the spring of 1982 they submitted a paper 'Light Rail in Manchester: The Complement to the Windsor Link?' It suggested converting six routes to light rail: the Bury line and Oldham Loop (both of L&YR origin) together with lines to Altrincham, Hadfield and Marple along with the rejuvenation of the former Midland main line as far as East Didsbury.

The system would join by rail, for the first time ever, Piccadilly and Victoria stations through the city streets and thus complement the Windsor Link concept. Passenger movement from any station in Greater Manchester to any other would be achieved by through train or one change only for the vast majority of journeys. Light rail would neatly lay alongside the Hazel Grove chord proposal by which BR's long distance services through the Peak District would be removed from the Marple route to serve Stockport, it would also bring passengers from the north via Victoria into Piccadilly to link with Manchester Airport should proposals for construction of a new line from Heald Green be approved. It is said that it took the PTE's formal Executive 10min to approve the report, whilst a further 10min meeting saw approval given to the commissioning of a full study by the consultants Mott, Hey & Anderson; but it took a further 10 years to bring Phase 1 of the scheme to fruition.

How the scheme progressed through that period is a long story involving consultation with BR, the various district councils in Greater Manchester and many other interested parties. It survived the dissolution of the county council and the deregulation of buses and also achieved the formal Parliamentary approval for the various and necessary Bills. Then in January 1988 the then Minister of Transport, David Mitchell, announced that grants could be available for the Metrolink Project if satisfactory tenders were received for private participation in the design, construction, maintenance and operation of the scheme. This moved it out of the public sector and into the private, much to the disappointment of those who had conceived the scheme and also to many commentators on the transport scene. A tendering process was initiated and in October 1989 the Government gave approval to Phase 1 of the project and work finally got underway.

Exactly two years later, on the morning of Sunday 15 September 1991, the first unit (No 1001) took to the city centre rails being propelled by a diesel shunter. Whether you call Metrolink a train or a super tram, its introduction marks another step in the development of the city's transport system, a story which has been well told in *Roads & Rails Of Manchester 1900-1950* (Ian Allan 1982).

A fleet of 26 modern two-car vehicles will operate the service, each set having a crush capacity of 270 passengers. The stations will be an interesting mixture of old and new, and a major improvement programme has been instituted to provide modern facilities with easy access for the less able. Information services are key aspects of Metrolink, and in addition to notice boards and an address system, a 'passenger assistance' button will enable a passenger in difficulty to speak with the control centre. There will also be closed-circuit TV surveillance systems, thereby offering greater security and fewer opportunities for vandalism etc. Stations will be equipped with at least two automatic ticket vending machines, but those who try and cheat the system will find themselves liable to be caught by ever vigilant supervisors. Though much is still to be completed, the conversion of the L&YR line to Metrolink has now been achieved.

Below:
Since the mid-1950s Heaton Park has witnessed dramatic changes. A whole generation of third-rail EMUs, the Class 504s, has come and gone; the third-rail itself has disappeared to be replaced by the overhead wires of the Metrolink scheme; and, attractive station canopies, so much a mark of the earlier photograph, have disappeared to be replaced by the functional buildings of the postwar years. At least Heaton Park has retained reasonable passenger facilities unlike so many other stations. The lighter section of the platform, where the intending passengers are waiting for the tram, has been painted to emphasise the point at which the tram will stop. After several delays, the Metrolink service started in early 1992.
Author

The West Riding

Halifax & District

Halifax is an industrial town of great character, and known nationally because of its building society — the largest in the world. In railway terms, however, it is less well-known. Though Halifax was under two miles from the M&L line at North Dean, it was situated in the Hebble Valley which was difficult for the main line to negotiate. A railhead was duly established on the main line at Elland and an active carting trade operated into Halifax. The provision of a branch into the town was considered shortly after the M&L opened in 1841, yet it was not until 1 July 1844 that the town was connected to the railway network. Even then, the facility that was provided was one of considerable annoyance to the residents of the area. Many of Halifax's traditional trade routes lay to the west, principally Manchester — yet, the branch made its junction with the M&L via an east-facing junction. In addition, the route was steeply graded and trains were subject to frequent delays as they slipped on the incline which was as steep as 1 in 45 in places.

The situation was to remain like this for some considerable time, and few significant improvements were made until the West Riding Union Railway was promoted jointly by the M&L and the Leeds & Bradford Railway.

The Bill for some 45½ miles of new railways was authorised in August 1846, promising a connection with the North Midland line at Bradford, as well as a more direct route to Leeds via Stanningley. As far as Halifax was concerned this scheme was of considerable benefit, primarily because it promised the long-awaited west-facing connection to the M&L. It would have a ruling gradient of 1 in 120, and leave the branch at Dryclough Junction just south of Halifax, joining the main line at Milner Royd Junction near Norland. The line was ready for inspection by the middle of 1851, but the opening was frustrated due to improvements needed for Sowerby Bridge station, and the cut-off route could not be inaugurated until 1 January 1852.

The second element of the West Riding extensions which concerned Halifax was a seven mile long line to Low Moor, where a junction would be made with the branch from Mirfield to Bradford. This was to be a difficult route to build, not least because of the 1,105yd-long tunnel to be cut through Beacon Hill just east of the town. A new station was built to replace the M&L terminus at Shaw Syke, but this was only to be a temporary measure and a more permanent station was planned. From Halifax the route climbed steeply up to Low Moor, necessitat-

Below right:
The powers to build the branch to Ripponden were obtained in 1865, but it was a further eight years before work began. The construction was attended by several difficulties and it took a full five years to complete; the line opened in the summer of 1878. The branch was envisaged as being the first stage in a short cut from the Calder Valley to Rochdale, involving a lengthy tunnel under the Pennines at Blackstone Edge. This scheme was of dubious value and was dropped due to financial considerations, though a later extension took the line up to Rishworth in 1881. In the first years of the 20th century a rebuilt Barton Wright 0-6-0ST, No 541, is seen running 'wrong line' at Watson's Crossing on an engineers' train, as a pointsman holds back the catch-point lever.
Real Photographs/Ian Allan Library

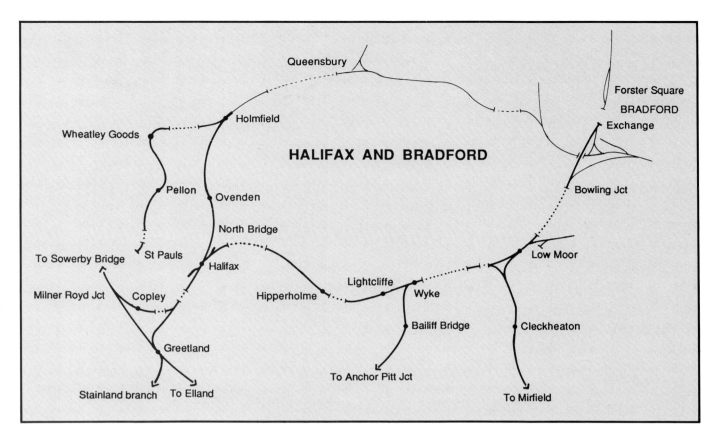

ing substantial viaducts, bridges, tunnels and earthworks to maintain a ruling gradient of 1 in 200. Following the opening of the Bradford-Low Moor line in May 1850, the link from Halifax went into operation on 7 August.

An important part of the development of Halifax's railway network were the branch lines which were to follow the main building programme, and these commenced with the 3¾ mile long branch from Greetland to Stainland which opened on 1 January 1857. There then came a lull of over 20 years, but this was followed by a frenzied period of activity commencing with the opening of a branch line up the Ryburn Valley from Sowerby Bridge. A year after the opening of the branch to Ripponden, a railway was to be driven north from Halifax to Holmfield. Opened by the Great Northern Railway in September 1879, it was extended to Queensbury three months later thus providing an

Left:
Regrettably, Halifax station is now nothing but a disgrace; its fine architecture and classic lines are spoiled by years of neglect. As a gateway to the town it is a very poor advert indeed; one of the islands has been completely removed and the main island with its superb buildings is completely derelict. Grand plans for a museum complex in the old GNR goods yard/warehouse were dealt a severe blow when receivers were appointed to wind up the affairs of the Museum of the Working Horse in the early summer of 1991. A few months later a Class 158 two-car DMU heads towards the station on a Liverpool-York working.
Martin Eltham

alternate service between Halifax and Bradford. The advent of this competition forced the L&YR to improve further its own services, and the two companies settled down to a mutually rewarding existence in the town. An example of this co-operation was noted in a magnificent joint station with three island platforms which was constructed on the site of the 'permanent' station of 1885. The co-operation did not extend to goods traffic, however, and each company had its own yards. The principle L&YR goods depot was at Shaw Syke, whilst the GNR's facilities were nearby just off South Parade.

A nominally independent company, the Halifax High Level Railway was opened in 1890 to serve the elevated residential and manufacturing suburbs of St Paul's and Pellon to the west of the town. This line made a junction with the GNR line at Holmfield, and ran to the terminus which was at

an altitude of over 300ft higher than the town's main station. The venture was taken over by the GNR and L&YR as a joint service, but passenger traffic was 'suspended' in 1917 — a casualty of the staff and locomotive shortages of World War 1! The next loss came in 1929, when competition from tram routes caused the withdrawal of passenger services to Rishworth in July and Stainland in September. Rishworth lost its goods trains in 1953 when they were cut back to terminate at Ripponden & Barkisland, and the branch closed entirely in September 1958. The line to Stainland fared little better and closed exactly 12 months later. The joint goods line to St Paul's remained operational until June 1960, although the passenger trains between Halifax and Holmfield had been withdrawn in 1955.

The widescale withdrawal of passenger services in the 1950s, followed by the savage pruning of the goods lines in the 1960s, has decimated Halifax's rail network. The only surviving passenger line is the route from Milner Royd Junction to Bradford, but it remains quite an attractive one on which to travel today. The original branch from Greetland is still intact but currently disused, though it has been retained in case a Wakefield or Huddersfield service can be reintroduced at some future date — an event which would lead to the reinstatement of stations at Brighouse and Elland. Just the pair of platforms that remain in use and a mass of rusted sidings illustrate what an important station Halifax once was. The line northeastwards from the town is totally devoid of intermediate stations; Hipperholme, Lightcliffe, Wyke & Norwood Green, and even the magnificent junction at Low Moor have all been swept away in two periods of carnage — 1963 and 1965-66. At the present time there are no immediate plans to restore stations between Halifax and Bradford, despite the growing population of the hinterland through which the line passes — particularly Hipperholme and Wyke where such a provision would seem to be a logical development. As the line descends towards Bradford there is one redeeming feature, as a sign at Low Moor proclaims this to be the projected site for the West Yorkshire Transport Museum which is due to open in 1994 and may pave the way for a new station at the former junction.

The Spen Valley Line

The first railway promoted through the Spen Valley was projected as part of a route to link Bradford to Manchester, paying little attention to local needs. As a link route it was much needed, for prior to its opening the only connection between Bradford and the M&L line was a horse-drawn bus service, which ran from the station at Brighouse. Progress was swift on the lower section of the line, and it opened between Mirfield and Low Moor on 18 July 1848. This line involved a stiff climb up to the high ground at Low Moor, and the five miles from Heckmondwike to the summit were at a ruling gradient of 1 in 100. Unfortunately the lengthy Bowling Tunnel delayed progress into Bradford, and the line did not open into the city for another 22 months.

Though the railway provided extensive facilities at all the major settlements in the Spen Valley, local traffic remained a secondary consideration for a very long time. Local business interests in the Spen Valley were gradually to receive a better service, but their main need was a for a direct service to Wakefield. Financial constraints precluded the building of a new line, so the L&YR put forward two compromise proposals. These would have allowed for the provision of an east-facing spur at Mirfield, followed by an inter-company link between the L&YR and the LNWR at Thornhill. Unfortunately the plan foundered, and the L&YR were forced to proceed with the Thornhill-Heckmondwike branch. A triangular junction was laid out at Thornhill, though the Bill of 17 June 1861 gave no authority to build the west facing arm. Despite the fact that the line was only 2¼ miles long with just one major bridge and a single intermediate station to construct, it was not completed until the spring of 1869. The slow progress leads one to conclude that the L&YR were not in a great hurry to provide the much needed direct route to Wakefield. Because of the poor services through the Spen Valley, the Midland and Great Northern railways were encouraged to offer competing services, but their plans were deflected by the L&YR's offer of running powers. Eventually the LNWR found its way into the Spen Valley, with the construction of a 'New Line' to Leeds, which was devised both to capture local traffic and to reduce congestion on the LD&M.

Below:
The West Yorkshire Transport Museum collection consists of some 40 trams, buses and trolleybuses, together with two electric locomotives. One of these is a 220V dc 4-wheel loco from Spondon Power Station, capable of running on either overhead or battery supplied power. The other is a 600V dc four-wheeled loco from Harton Colliery, South Shields. The museum also owns a Class 506 EMU and the unique battery-electric railcar set used on the Aberdeen-Ballater branch (later at the BR Research Laboratory in Derby), but following the enforced move from Hammerton Street diesel depot (pictured here) both of these are now stored away from the site.
West Yorkshire Transport Museum

Grouping did not directly affect services through the Spen Valley, but nationalisation brought the slow demise of both lines. In October 1953, British Railways withdrew the Huddersfield-Leeds 'stopping' trains leaving the LNWR line for express working. Within four years, the Thornhill-Bradford trains had gone, and despite the introduction of DMUs the Thornhill-Heckmondwike trains lasted only until 1962, then both routes completely lost their passenger status in June 1965, with the Mirfield-Heckmondwike section closing completely. However, the Thornhill-Low Moor section was retained, providing a direct freight link between Bradford and Healey Mills. In 1966 the 'New Line' closed completely but, in order to allow access to Heckmondwike Goods Yard, a spur was built to the old L&YR route. The construction of the M62 trans-Pennine motorway caused consid-

erable disruption to the line, and it closed for a period during this time, reopening in 1974 complete with a new viaduct constructed at considerable expense by the Department of Transport. Though the L&YR line was thus left intact, the need for the service was diminishing due to BR's freight policies and in 1981 the section between Heckmondwike and Bradford was closed. Finally the section south of Heckmondwike closed in the late 1980s with the loss of the contract to deliver oil to a terminal at Liversedge.

The West Yorkshire Transport Museum

The West Yorkshire Transport Museum Trust was founded by the former West Yorkshire Metropolitan County Council in 1984, as part of a strategy to establish a number of major new museum projects in the county. The development was conceived on a massive

scale, including the reopening of the Spen Valley line as an electric tramway. Twenty-six acres of land were obtained at Low Moor on the former L&YR site, along with 5½ miles of the old line through Cleckheaton. However, before any start could be made on the project, the development was abruptly halted by the abolition of the County Council in April 1986. There then followed two years of legal wrangling over the future of the Trust and of the ownership of the land, during which time the museum plans were shelved. But in 1988 a new Board of Trustees was appointed, and a new strategy evolved on

very strict commercial criteria. The new Transport Centre approach will have a strong private sector involvement, which reflects the changing world that all museums now face.

The new project will be a working museum, developed on the former L&YR goods yard at Low Moor, and the GNR Dudley Hill-Low Moor spur. Rather than being a collection of static exhibits, it is intended to demonstrate the operation of trams, trains, trolleybuses and diesel buses. The buses will operate on a route from the car park to Cleckheaton Road bridge, while trains will run as far as Oakenshaw Tunnel.

WAKEFIELD

Methley

Castleford

Methley Joint

To Pontefract

Normanton

Goosehill Jct

Wakefield Westgate

Wakefield Kirkgate

A

Oakenshaw

To Featherstone

Sharlston

B

Crofton

To Horbury

A loco shed
B Oakenshaw Junction

To Ryhill

There are, as yet, no plans for the development of the Spen Valley line, though it is envisaged that this will eventually form part of a preserved electric railway. Meanwhile a collection of vehicles has been assembled at the former Ludlam Street depot in Bradford, and these can be inspected any Sunday for a modest fee.

In early 1992 it was announced that the West Yorkshire Transport Museum Trust had been awarded a multi-million pound grant by the government. This dramatic improvement in the Museum's fortunes has ensured that the first phase of the development plan will now be pushed through.

Bradford

The L&YR had a hard job to reach Bradford, and they were beaten to the task by the Leeds & Bradford Railway (North Midland Railway) who reached the city via Shipley in 1846. Even so, the real benefits were to be experienced by the railway which provided a route to the west, the direction in which many of Bradford's commercial links lay. This became the declared objective of the M&L but they struggled with their line up the Spen Valley, and by 1848 it had only got as far a Low Moor. The branch was eventually continued on to Bradford in May 1850, and three months later it was supplemented by the line from Halifax. A direct route to Leeds from Bradford was the next logical development and such a scheme was duly promoted by the West Riding Union, and therefore a protégé of the M&L. Unfortunately the construction difficulties on the other sections of the WRU had resulted in an extreme shortage of cash, and as a consequence powers were sought for abandoning the Leeds direct

Below right:
The imposing terminus of Bradford Exchange was opened in 1887-88 and was shared between the L&YR and the Great Northern. The L&YR had reached Bradford in 1850 and the railway's first station was at Drake Street at the foot of the 1 in 50 gradient leading to Bowling tunnel. This was extended to become a joint station with the GNR in 1867, but the facilities were inadequate and from the early 1870s work progressed culminating with the completion of the new station. One of the Aspinall-designed Atlantics is seen waiting to depart from Bradford Exchange. The design was reminiscent of King's Cross — the GNR's other imposing terminus — and the station was only slightly narrower than the London terminus.
Ian Allan Library

Bottom right:
In later years Bradford Exchange became an increasingly depressing station with much of the glazing from the roof removed in the late 1960s and with many of the train services withdrawn. Seen on 20 June 1970 the great station had less than three years to go before closure. Undoubtedly the decimation of Bradford's local railway network made the 10 platforms of Exchange unnecessary, but this was compounded by the apparent lack of maintenance. When, in the early 1970s, problems developed with the Bridge Street overbridge (a bridge which crossed the station throat), the opportunity was taken to redevelop a new station south of the road bridge and close the existing terminus. After closure in 1973 the bulk of the station was demolished, with the exception of the offices and roof over the concourse area; these survived until 1977 when the new office accommodation linked into the Interchange was completed. After more than a decade as a car park, the station site is now occupied by the new law courts.
N. E. Preedy

Left:
**The modern Bradford
Exchange (or Interchange as
it has now become called) is
but a pale shadow of the
former station. Opened in
January 1973 when the old
Exchange closed, the new
station 'boasts' four
platforms, of which only
three are now regularly used
for passenger trains.
Although perceived originally
as the city's InterCity station,
these trains have now been
diverted to a revitalised and
rebuilt Forster Square.
Adjacent to the new station,
and one of the factors in its
building, is the massive bus
station, which was built on
the site of the L&YR Bridge
Street goods shed.**
Author

route. However, the Leeds, Bradford & Halifax Joint Railway stepped into the breach in 1852, and by 1 August 1854 their line had opened to a terminus in Adolphus Street. Though the LB&HJR was later to be absorbed by the GNR, it gave the L&YR the opportunity of running through to Leeds. The provision of a spur from the WRU to the LB&HJR at Bowling Junction provided the facility for direct running which was much quicker way to Leeds than the original route via Mirfield, Wakefield and Normanton.

However, looking at Bradford's railways today, I wonder if all the hard effort and work was really worth it — I am sure that if the promoters came back today they certainly would not approve! In January 1867 the city's new station opened on the site of the L&YR terminus, whilst the GNR station became a goods depot. The Midland (L&B) station was just a tantalising few streets away, and a link

between the two could easily have been provided. In fact, after the failure of the original M&L/L&B scheme in 1846, there were repeated attempts to make the connection but all failed to materialise. The L&YR/GNR station was greatly improved in the 1880s, after which it became known as Exchange, but sadly Bradford was to remain served by what were effectively three long branch lines, and the situation remains the same today. Yet, strange to relate, when I worked in Bradford in the early 1970s my office block was still owned by the British Rail Property Board, as were a large number of other properties on a line between Exchange and Forster Square stations — a legacy of the once ambitious plans.

Regrettably, the opportunity to link the two stations was finally lost when the magnificent Exchange station was closed on 14 January 1973, its replacement being situated on the

Below left:
**The acquisition of the H&SJR
and the associated branch
line to Holmfirth left the
M&L with a 15-mile section
which was totally
disconnected from the rest of
their system. Access to
Huddersfield had to be
gained over the H&M line
from Heaton Lodge Junction,
but only at the cost of
granting the LNWR running
powers between Heaton
Lodge and Thornhill. In
Huddersfield a magnificent
joint station was built and,
though grime-stained and
covered in pigeon droppings,
this 1950 view still reveals its
architectural merit. The line
through the station to
Springwood Junction was
also jointly owned, obviating
the need for an expensive
duplication of tunnels
through the sandstone ridge
to the west of the town. The
former L&YR booking office,
in the wing nearest the
camera, has recently been
restored and developed for
commercial use.**
Huddersfield Newspapers Group

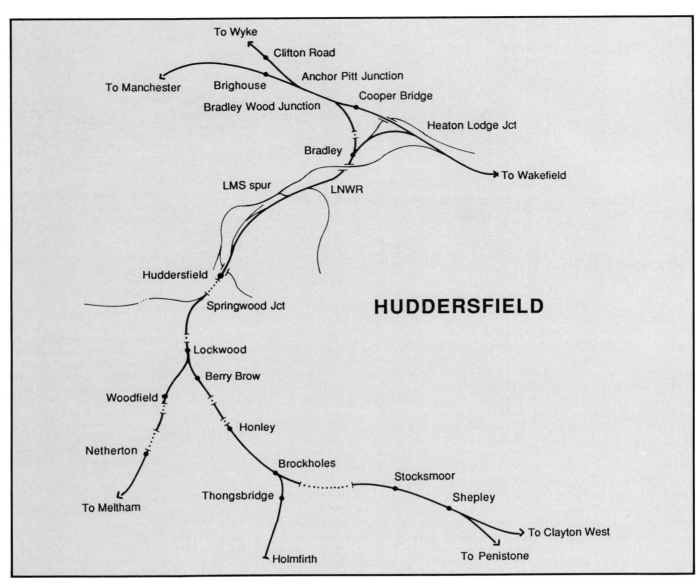

To Wyke
Clifton Road
Anchor Pitt Junction
To Manchester
Brighouse
Cooper Bridge
Bradley Wood Junction
Heaton Lodge Jct
Bradley
LMS spur
LNWR
To Wakefield
Huddersfield

HUDDERSFIELD

Springwood Jct
Lockwood
Berry Brow
Woodfield
Honley
Netherton
Brockholes
Stocksmoor
Shepley
To Meltham
Thongsbridge
To Clayton West
To Penistone
Holmfirth

Right:
The magnificent joint station at Huddersfield must still rank as the finest provincial railway building in Britain, particularly after the extensive restoration of the façade was completed in 1991. However, the interior remains something of an anti-climax as evidence in this 23 March 1991 picture of the station's east end bays. Neville Hill-based Class 156, No 156448, waits to depart on the 12.59 stopping train to Wakefield, despite displaying a Leeds destination blind.
Author

west side of Bridge Street where a combined bus/coach/railway station was to be built, further lengthening the gap between the two stations. Rejoicing in the name Bradford Interchange, its title belied what was really needed for the city — a through rail route. Just four dead-end platforms formed the new station, and today only three are regularly in use for the intensive service from Leeds to Bradford as well as the York-Manchester/ Liverpool and Blackpool trains which continue through Halifax to join the Calder Valley at Milner Royd. The fourth platform is usually occupied by parcels/mail stock, a much needed facility due to the fact that all of the city's numerous goods depots have now disappeared. The concrete monolith of the Interchange is already showing signs of decay, but the lower concourse is bright and cheerful with shops, providing a welcome change to the bleak railway platforms and the hangar-like bus terminus.

The Huddersfield & Sheffield Junction Railway

Though the M&L had already developed a route over the Pennines, its meandering line via Summit could hardly be called a direct one. The more logical choice was to cross the Pennines at Standedge, and the company had a branch line from Manchester to Stalybridge which could have provided the first stage in a direct route. Unfortunately, this option was not taken as the M&L seemed to have a great reluctance in building a through route via Standedge and Huddersfield. Though there was rich traffic to be captured in the area, the only provision they made for the Huddersfield district was a station on the main line at Cooper Bridge, some considerable distance from the town centre.

Eventually the M&L offered to run a branch line into Huddersfield, but it was surveyed to follow the line of the Sir John Ramsden's Canal along the valley floor. This would have terminated at Aspley on the south side of the town, from where it would have been difficult to extend westward. Totally disenchanted with the M&L, local people promoted their own lines. The first was the Huddersfield & Manchester Railway & Canal Co, which was to run from the joint Sheffield, Ashton & Manchester Railway/Manchester & Leeds Railway station at Stalybridge, to a junction with the M&L at Heaton Lodge just west of Cooper Bridge. The second was promoted to join the SA&MR at Penistone and thus provide a direct route to Sheffield. This gave the SA&MR a unique opportunity to absorb the independent companies and thus gain access to Huddersfield. However, an extraordinary period of negotiation, collusion and intrigue followed. The Huddersfield people felt that their interests would be better served by forming an alliance with the companies supporting railway development in the West Riding, and this led to the M&L gaining control of the H&SJR and the LNWR absorbing the H&M, whilst the poor old SA&MR got nothing.

When the H&SJR and the associated branch to Holmfirth opened on 1 July 1850, the L&YR did not have sufficient locomotives to work the line in its entirety, and they entered into an unusual arrangement with the SA&MR. This resulted in the L&YR running trains from Huddersfield to Holmfirth, whilst the SA&MR ran a service from Penistone to Holmfirth. Both services passed through Brockholes Junction where an interchange was made. Regrettably the connections were so inadequate, the service received a great deal of criticism and the M&L's name was once again brought into disrepute locally. In due course the M&L became the L&YR, and a gradual improvement was seen from about 1861-62 onwards. Two branch lines were promoted from the H&SJR in the 1860s, to Meltham and Clayton West, but both were to prove very difficult to build. The first train ran along the 3¾ mile Meltham Branch on 8 August 1868, but a series of land-slips

Above left:

To the south of Huddersfield, the L&YR operated a number of branch lines; these ran to the small towns of Meltham, Holmfirth and Clayton West. The Holmfirth branch, like that to Clayton West, was the subject of several extension proposals, none of which materialised. When these were finally ruled out by the L&YR, they built a superb station building for the single platform terminus. Pictured at the attractive terminus of Holmfirth is Ivatt 2-6-2T No 41250.
Author's Collection

Above:

The branch from Brockholes to Holmfirth closed to passenger services on 2 November 1959. More than 30 years on it is difficult to imagine that a railway operated to this point. Part of the station remains, however, evinced by the chimneys of the station master's house, although the platform accommodation (including canopies) has long gone. The platform has been levelled and on its site a Kingdom Hall has been erected. Remarkably this stone-built church was put up in just 48hr by an army of 2,500 volunteers.
Author

between Meltham Junction and Netherton resulted in the line being closed on 1 October. A number of substantial retaining walls were duly built and the line reopened on 5 July 1869. The next development was the Clayton West line, which was also delayed by constructional problems and did not open until August 1879. The Meltham branch had no less than four intermediate stations, though one lasted only for a month. The lines to Holmfirth and Clayton West had only one intermediate stop each — Thongsbridge and Skelmanthorpe respectively, but it was hoped to convert and extend both branches into through lines. Clayton West was repeatedly (but unsuccessfully) projected towards Barnsley, whilst the Holmfirth branch had grand plans of making a connection with the Woodhead line, though in the end even the lesser objective of a terminus at Holmbridge failed to succeed.

Local services were well patronised, and the three branch lines all produced satisfying traffic returns. This remained the situation up to the end of World War 2, but shortly afterwards improved local bus services (jointly owned by the LMS) began to make serious inroads into local passenger traffic. The Meltham Branch lost its passenger service in

May 1949, but it continued to handle substantial goods traffic particularly tractor trains. Diesel multiple units were introduced on services between Huddersfield and Penistone and the Clayton West branch in November 1959. Unfortunately Holmfirth lost its passenger trains at the same time. In 1965 local freight services were withdrawn from all the intermediate stations on the H&SJR, and the Holmfirth and Meltham branches closed completely. In the early/mid-1960s the main line status was firstly downgraded to a secondary route and then completely withdrawn, and by 1969 the route had been singled between Denby Dale and Penistone. A repeated battle was waged to save the line from the Beeching era onwards, and for years it remained perilously positioned. Eventually the Passenger Transport Authorities of West and South Yorkshire agreed on a compromise to save the line, which involved rerouteing trains from Huddersfield to Sheffield via the Penistone-Barnsley line. Unfortunately, this rerouteing also coincided with the closure of the Clayton West branch and the section of the former Woodhead line between Penistone to Stocksbridge on 24 January 1983.

The Clayton West Branch/Kirklees Light Railway

Though the Clayton West branch was vigorously promoted as the first part of a through route to Barnsley, the L&YR appear to have had no pressing urgency to build it. The proposals were probably designed as a means to prevent the LNWR building their own route to the South Yorkshire coalfield, and even when construction eventually began the progress was terribly slow. Though the first sod was cut on 27 November 1872, the L&YR repeatedly had to ask for extensions to the fixed time limit and it was not ready for inspection until 29 July 1879. In the three and a half miles there was just one intermediate station, Skelmanthorpe. At both stations there were large sidings serving the neighbouring collieries which provided traffic right

Left:
The branch to Clayton West, serving as it did a number of collieries as well as the passenger stations, was to survive more than 20 years longer than its neighbouring branch lines. A three-car DMU waits at the increasingly derelict station at Clayton West on 30 March 1981 prior to its return to Huddersfield. The Clayton West branch was sacrificed as part of the deal which saw passenger services retained on the Huddersfield-Sheffield (via Penistone) route and the line closed to passengers on 24 January 1983. With the decline in the coal industry, freight services did not last much longer and the line was closed completely. After closure the track was left intact for a couple of years before it was eventually lifted and this could have been the end for the last of the traditional L&YR branches.
Barry Edwards

up to the final years of the line. However, it was declining coal traffic more than changes in local passenger traffic trends that gave justification for the branch to be axed and the end came on 24 January 1983.

After a gap of some seven years, a new railway was laid on the old track-bed using 15in gauge track. The Kirklees Light Railway Co currently runs a mile of single track line from Clayton West to Cuckoo's Nest Halt near Scissett, but it is envisaged that a double track will eventually run all the way to the former junction. In September 1991 the scheme received its Light Railway Order, and two days before delivering the manuscript of this book to the Ian Allan offices in Shepperton, the author was privileged to have an 'exclusive' ride on one of the 'first' steam trains from Clayton West. As the book goes to print the railway has entered its first full season, and is proving to be a popular tourist attraction. Three locomotives (two steam and one diesel) operate the service to Cuckoo's Nest as the PW gang heads towards Skelmanthorpe. Meanwhile, at Clayton West a visitor/tourist complex is being built to include a miniature village, boating lake, and a display of mill engines.

Below left:
Fortunately, the trackbed of the Clayton West branch was taken over for conversion into the 15in narrow gauge Kirklees Light Railway. With the old station building in the background, one of the light railway's engines waits at one of the specially constructed platforms. Although only running a short distance at present, it is the intention that the light railway will eventually run to the former BR junction near Shepley & Shelley on the Penistone line.
Author

8

Gateway to Europe and the Coalfields

Wakefield, Pontefract & Goole Railway

With the advent of the M&L line to Normanton, a new era opened up for the districts east of Wakefield which were predominantly associated with the mining of coal. Traditional transport links had been by a system of navigable rivers and canals that led to the River Ouse below Selby, which had seen the establishment of a port at Goole in the late 17th century. The desire for a railway linking the mining districts with the port appeared shortly after the opening of the Stockton & Darlington Railway, but it was not until 1845 that Parliamentary approval was received for the Wakefield, Pontefract & Goole Railway. This was to form a junction with the M&L at Wakefield, curve south and east to Crofton then pass through Featherstone, Pontefract, Knottingley, and Snaith before reaching Goole. Work began on 24 September 1845 and progressed steadily, but before the line opened on 29 March 1848 it had become part of the L&YR empire.

At Goole the L&YR terminus was alongside the Railway Dock, where two long platforms (with a 100ft-long overall roof) were situated adjacent to St John's Street. Branches led to a high-level coal drop and other parts of the dock. The growing importance of the port and town soon led to rival railways casting envious eyes at the area, and in the early 1860s the NER sponsored a line from Staddlethorpe to the South Yorkshire Railway at Thorne. This was simultaneous to the L&YR's Doncaster, Goole & Hull Junction Railway proposal, and though only the NER scheme received approval, the L&YR were awarded running powers into Hull in 1863. However, it would not appear as though these were exercised until a full year after the NER line opened in August 1869.

With access to the Humber the L&YR took an active share in the Hull Docks along with NER, LNWR and MS&LR companies from 1874 until 1893, when the NER assumed complete control. In 1881-82 the docks at

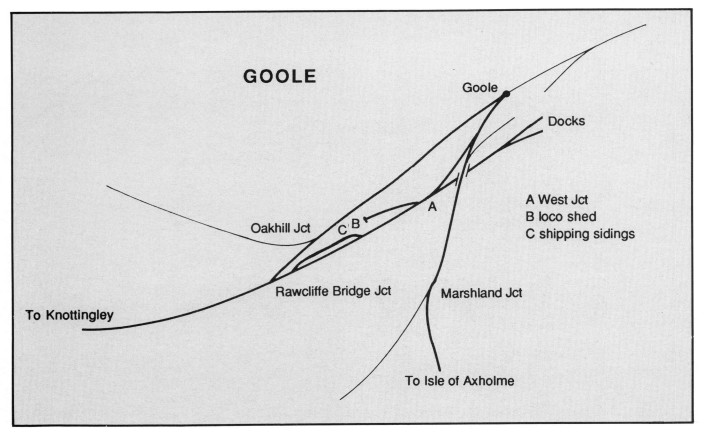

GOOLE

Goole

Docks

Oakhill Jct

A

C B

A West Jct
B loco shed
C shipping sidings

Rawcliffe Bridge Jct

Marshland Jct

To Knottingley

To Isle of Axholme

Goole were extended, and in anticipation of this the old WP&GR terminal closed in 1879 and the L&YR trains began using the NER station. Around the same time coal tippling (discharging) equipment was erected at the Railway and Stanhope docks, and in 1884-5 a new goods yard was laid out to meet the growing needs of the port. Also in 1885, a link was established from the WP&GR to the newly opened Hull & Barnsley line where the two crossed at Hensall, the spur eventually giving rise to a Hull-Knottingley service. Meanwhile the traffic to Hull over the NER line had expanded significantly, so the L&YR catered for this by opening their own goods shed in Hull and stabling locomotives at the NER engine shed from 1886.

In 1906 the L&YR introduced a new express service from Liverpool to Hull which connected with the steamers to Zeebrugge, from where Belgian State Railways took over. In 1910 a new NER line from Selby joined the Goole-Doncaster line at Boothferry Road Junction, and a spur was opened from the L&YR at Rawcliffe Bridge Junction and all L&YR passenger traffic was diverted this way from 1 May 1912. The section from Rawcliffe Bridge Junction down to Goole West Junction remained very busy with freight traffic to the docks, largely because of the L&YR's shipping interest in the port. The Goole Steamship Co had been established in 1864 after the failure of the long-established firm of Watson, Cunliffe & Co,

the first GSC boat being *The Walter Stanhope*, purchased in 1865 after an interesting career as blockade runner for the Confederate States of America Navy. From 1884 the company took to naming its boats after Yorkshire rivers, the first being *Ouse* built on the Tyne by William Dobson & Co. In 1895 the company purchased the Hull Steamship Co but in turn the GSC was acquired by the L&YR who took control from 1 January 1905.

The final piece of railway development was a short, east-facing curve from the Askern branch at Knottingley on to the WP&GR, which opened in 1915 and has the distinction of being the last piece of railway built by the L&YR. In 1935, the LMS allowed the Goole Steamship Co to merge with Associated Humber Lines and an era passed as the continental market suffered from the Depression. The railway remained busy, principally with export coal traffic, and this position continued up to World War 2. The war years were important for both Goole and its railway, but in the 1950s traditional freight flows began to fall away. New avenues opened, however, as the flat Yorkshire countryside saw the construction of several huge electricity generating stations. On 2 January 1967 the Wakefield-Goole passenger trains were withdrawn and replaced by a Leeds-Castleford-Knottingley-Goole service. This still operates, but its frequency east of Knottingley is so scandalous that the couple of trains each day are hardly worth bothering about. Even so, the journey

Below:
The WP&GR had a distinctive architectural style, and a series of very attractive stations were erected at Featherstone, Pontefract, Knottingley, Whitley Bridge, Hensall, Snaith and Rawcliffe. In the years that followed additional stations were opened at Crofton, Sharlston (both 1853) and Tanshelf (1873). This view at Whitley Bridge probably dates from around the turn of the century, looking over the level crossing towards the station buildings.
B. C. Lane Collection

Right:

In July 1965 a new line was opened from the WP&GR to Ferrybridge power station, while just 12 months later a second new line provided a connection from the railway at Whitley Bridge to another generating station at Eggborough. In the 1990s, the WP&GR is now almost entirely the preserve of MGR trains operating to the many power stations in the district with the majority being worked by locomotives from the Knottingley depot. On 27 July 1989 a grimy Class 56, No 56110, works an empty MGR from Drax through Whitley Bridge *en route* to Allerton Bywater colliery. The station buildings are now gone, but the level crossing and box both remain.
John Bateman

Below right:

Originally promoted by two companies — the Goole & Marshland Light Railway Railway and the Isle of Axholme Light Railway — at the end of the 19th century an Act of 1902 empowered the L&YR and North Eastern Railway jointly to take over and operate the projected lines under the title of the Axholme Joint Railway. The lines were completed in 1909. Regular passenger services were operated over the 27¾-mile system (with the exception of the Hatfield branch) until 1933. Taken over by the LMS and LNER in 1923, the Axholme Joint received its first Sentinel steam car in 1926; a second and larger Sentinel was acquired in 1930. This vehicle is pictured at Crowle. Numbered 44, it was a rare example of a joint line possessing its own motive power. After the closure of the Axholme Joint, it passed to the LNER and was withdrawn in 1944. The Axholme Joint's freight services continued after the passenger closure; the last section, from Marshland Junction to Belton, being retained until the early 1970s as a private siding for the CEGB.
Real Photographs/Ian Allan Library

from Castleford to Goole is well worth travelling, with the station at Hensall being the highlight of the trip. The station house is complete with an attractive Victorian post box, stained glass L&YR doors, enamelled signs and a vintage Fowler traction engine — which can occasionally be seen steaming in the goods yard. The other stations are all extant, but in various stages of decay.

Meanwhile the WP&GR is alive with Merry-Go-Round (MGR) trains, mostly operated by locomotives from the Knottingley depot. The track remains double as far as Hensall Junction (where a curve has been proposed onto the Selby - Doncaster line), then it splits with a single track continuing to Goole and another running on the former Hull & Barnsley line as far as Drax Power Station. Knottingley retains its station, but this is a basic timber-built affair. Meanwhile in May 1992 a new Wakefield-Knottingley service was reintroduced, along with new stations at Pontefract (Tanshelf), Featherstone and Streethouse.

The Askern Branch

When the WP&GR was authorised, it was also empowered to build three branches one of which, the Methley Branch, ran to the north side of the line and is discussed in the following section. The other two were connecting lines to the south, the first of these being the short but exceptionally useful spur on to the North Midland line at Oakenshaw. The second was a much longer line and it diverged from the WP&GR at Knottingley and ran for 10 miles to Askern Junction, where an end-on connection would be made with the Great Northern branch from Doncaster. While work on the Oakenshaw branch proceeded in fits and starts before being suspended in August 1848 (in fact it did not open until July 1861), work on the line to Askern had been completed that June. Intermediate stations were established at Womersley, Norton and Askern in sparsely populated farming districts, but the real benefit of the line was not seen to lie in the carriage of local traffic. At this time there was still no main line up the East Coast, and for a while the Askern branch became an important part in the development of that route.

While coal traffic has been the staple business on the line since its conception, by contrast the passenger services fared badly after the NER line opened as it was served by little

Below:
At Goole the engine shed and goods yard have long been removed, and the Renault car terminal has also recently closed. It is interesting to note that from the former Rawcliffe Bridge Junction today's route follows the original L&YR line to Boothferry Road via Goole West Junction. The lines down to the docks are still used, but rusting tracks testify that traffic is nowhere near as extensive as it once was. On 25 June 1989 No 37241 stands on almost deserted sidings, accompanied by two Class 08 shunters, but with just one solitary freight vehicle in sight the supply of motive power seems excessive!
John Bateman

Right:

The northward projection of the GNR worried the infamous George Hudson, and he obtained powers to construct a line from the Y&NMR at Burton Salmon to the WP&GR at Knottingley and then have power to run down the Askern branch into Doncaster. The GNR were allowed to run into York via this route when it opened in 1850, and thus this branch of the L&YR became part of the first ECML. This status remained intact until 1871, when the NER line opened between Chaloner Whin Junction at York and Shaftholme Junction just south of Askern. By BR days the Askern branch had mainly become a trunk route for coal traffic, and on 14 June 1957 a representative scene is captured at Womersley as ex-WD 2-8-0 No 90651 heads a coal train from Askern or Bentley to Crofton.
P. Cookson

Right:

The L&YR's only pretension towards serving London was also connected with this branch, for, in 1864, it formed part of a joint L&YR/GER proposal for a 113-mile line from Askern to Cambridge via Lincoln and Peterborough — sadly this Bill was defeated in its second reading in Parliament, though by only 41 votes. The L&YR branch remains open primarily for the conveyance of coal, a traffic which seems safe enough though Askern colliery has now closed. In August 1991 the attractive station house at Womersley is pictured over the level crossing. Though the passenger service no longer remains, we can be grateful that such architectural gems have been retained.
Author

more than local trains. While ever a degree of railway competition was encouraged the services were safe, but, just prior to nationalisation, all the stations on the branch closed in March 1947. The few remaining express workings were sent by other routes and the only passenger trains that then traversed the 'branch' were specials or diversions. The local goods service was withdrawn in 1964-65, but the line still had an important traffic in coal. Today it remains a useful link from South Yorkshire to the coal-fired power stations to the north, but at the end of 1991 the short spur off the branch serving the colliery at Askern ceased operations when coal production ended. The other branch is also intact, and from the west junction at Crofton it still connects the WP&GR to the former Midland system, but that line is now truncated and runs only as far south as Houghton Main — meanwhile at Crofton East Junction a short spur leads to a Civil Engineering depot.

The Methley Branch

The north facing branch off the WP&GR ran from Pontefract to Methley with just one intermediate station at Castleford. However, this branch was not particularly aimed at local traffic and was more by way of a connection on to other railway systems. In 1836 the M&L had obtained running powers over the North Midland into Leeds, and by making the junction with this line at Methley the WP&GR obtained a west-facing route into that city. The contract for construction was let in 1846, but various delays meant that it was not ready until September 1848 when excursion trains first ran from Leeds to Doncaster in connection with the St Leger race meeting. It was opened to goods traffic in December and in April 1850 the L&YR introduced a regular passenger service between Pontefract and Leeds via Methley Junction. A connection from the L&YR line at Cutsyke Junction curved round on to the NER line from Milford to Normanton, meeting it just west of Castleford New station and forming the basis for a useful Castleford-Pontefract service when the line opened in the late 1870s.

The second development from Methley was a joint railway (GNR/L&YR/NER) which ran to a triangular junction with the GNR at Lofthouse, which not only provided a second route into Leeds but gave one which was completely independent of the Midland Railway. Passenger traffic on the line was commenced in July 1869 by the GNR, but coal was the main flow of L&YR traffic along this useful artery. As L&YR passenger services were mainly routed via the Midland line it is sufficient to say that the GNR/LNER's service on the Methley Joint served a useful purpose, but by the time it had been withdrawn in 1964 it had largely become a local working to Pontefract via Castleford. Severe mining subsidence affected the line's 'freight only' prospects and it closed in April 1965, with only a short section being left at the eastern end to serve colliery traffic, though even that had finished by the early 1970s.

Meanwhile the Methley branch is still carrying both passengers and freight, but the section between Whitwood and Castleford junctions has been removed. Passenger trains from Leeds run into the ex-NER station at Castleford along the old Midland route via Woodlesford, then reverse out of the station and down the curve to Cutsyke and the site of the old L&YR station. From there they pass through mining-ravaged countryside to Pontefract Monkhill Goods Junction, and into Monkhill station. Pontefract still has two sta-

tions, with Baghill on the former Swinton & Knottingley Joint Railway (MR/NER) still serving a useful function, though the useful curve between this line and the WP&GR which opened in 1879 no longer exists. Meanwhile, the section of the WP&GR west of Pontefract, which has been devoid of regular passenger trains for two decades, has at last seen the introduction of a PTE-supported passenger service to Wakefield.

Into The Coal Field

In the 1840s a branch was envisaged from the H&SJR at Shepley to run to Barnsley via Clayton West, and this could be conceived as the first plan to capture the South Yorkshire coal traffic, albeit by a rather circuitous route. Though the H&SJR eventually became part of the L&YR which received authority to build a line to Barnsley, no progress was ever made east of Clayton West. In 1846 the Sheffield, Rotherham, Barnsley, Wakefield, Huddersfield & Goole Railway was authorised to build a line from a junction with the Sheffield & Rotherham Railway to a double junction with the M&L at Horbury.

It was envisaged that the entire line would be leased to the M&L, but at the company's first AGM in October 1846 it was decided to give the section south of Barnsley to the South Yorkshire, Doncaster & Goole Railway, while the line northwards was let to the M&L along with the Silkstone Branch. Work on what was now referred to as the M&L's Barnsley Branch commenced in March 1847, but the following January the contractor was asked to reduce his costs and it was decided to cut back the works to a single track formation. However, this short-sighted decision, influenced by the lack of finance, left the single bore tunnel at Woolley as a major impediment to smooth traffic flows for many years to come. On 1 January 1850 the passenger services began, with the all-important freight (coal) trains commencing a fortnight later. Intermediate stations from Barnsley were at Darton, Haigh and Crigglestone, but the Silk-

Left:
In the twilight of its years an ex-L&YR 'A' class 0-6-0 No 52244 heads a 13-vehicle evening Goole-Wakefield pick-up goods passing milepost 36 between Knottingley and Pontefract (Monkhill) East Junction. At this time the trip would probably have terminated at Crofton sidings, once the area's major marshalling yard.
P. Cookson

Right:
Situated at the heart of the Yorkshire coalfield, Castleford was a magnet to the pre-Grouping railway companies. The L&YR served the town with a line from Methley Junction to Pontefract (Monkhill). With the post-Nationalisation rationalisation, the stretch of the L&YR from Methley Junction to Cutsyke Junction (including the ex-L&YR station) has been closed. Although not on the L&YR, this shot of the ex-NER station at Castleford is included as it allows comparison with the next shot, which illustrates the nature of the current operation over the ex-L&YR line to Goole from Leeds. In September 1958 'N1' No **69450** waits to leave Castleford with a train for Leeds.
P. Cookson

Right:
Since the closure of many of the lines north of the WP&GR, the passenger service from Knottingley (and the infrequent extension to Goole) now runs to Leeds via Castleford (New) station. This takes it down the Methley branch as far as the former Cutsyke Junction and then on the spur up to the former NER line, where it reverses, runs down to Whitwood Junction, curves round to Methley Junction, and then follows the former North Midland line into Leeds. On **21 April 1987** a Class **141** in the then green/cream livery of West Yorkshire PTA pulls out of Castleford on the **14.22** to Knottingley. Although the signal box, goods shed and semaphore signals remain from 30 years earlier, much else has disappeared.
John Bateman

stone branch and the short line down to the old canal basin were almost exclusively limited to freight. By 1853 the traffic in coal for Goole was so extensive that doubling was authorised, and with the exception of the 1,750yd-long Woolley Tunnel a second track opened throughout in the spring of 1855.

In 1851 the troubled South Yorkshire Railway section south of Barnsley had opened to form a through route, and from June their trains began running into the L&YR station. In January 1858 the L&YR purchased the northern section outright, and in June that year the MS&LR line from Penistone was opened into Barnsley. With this the L&YR decided to enlarge Barnsley station and recover part of the cost by charging the other companies tolls on their trains, but the cost appears to have been a little excessive and the matter was referred to the Railway Com-

missioners in 1859 and again in 1861. The matter was finally resolved in 1864, after the SYR had been acquired by the MS&LR, and the station became jointly owned. In 1870 the Midland opened its line into the town, and the MS&LR then moved its trains into the new Court House station. One could hardly blame them, for the L&YR station was something of a hovel, and even after substantial improvements the single platform 'low-level' station remained a disgrace. Directly opposite the main platform was the engine shed, jointly shared by the L&YR/MS&LR (later GCR). The LMS maintained a presence here until the 1930s, after which it became a pure LNER shed principally occupied by engines of GCR origins until it was demolished in the late 1950s.

The station remained one-sided until the closure of Court House was approved at the

end of 1959, and from 1960 all passengers services were diverted into an enlarged Exchange station. As the book goes to press a new interchange station nears completion, with a modern bus station being erected on the south side of the line partially on the old engine shed site. A magnificent new building has been erected on the Sheffield-bound platform, and though of modern design it blends sympathetically with the older buildings on the down side. North of Barnsley the double track runs to Darton, where a basic station serves as a common boundary for the West Yorkshire and South Yorkshire PTEs. Haigh station closed in 1965, but a siding still serves the large colliery nearby and MGR trains form a common scene on the line. Woolley Tunnel, finally doubled in 1902, still has both single bores in use. Crigglestone also closed in 1965, but it fared better than its neighbouring station on the Midland line from Thornhill to Cudworth (where the L&YR had running powers) which never saw regular passenger

services from its opening up to the time it was completely lifted after closure in 1964. At Horbury a forked junction was made with the M&L main line, but the west-facing arm of this line (opened in 1902) is under threat of closure at the time of writing, which is a great shame in view of the access it offers to Healey Mills. Passenger services have remained reasonably useful since the conversion to DMU operation, with occasional fluctuations into the abysmal zone, but from 1992 further enhancements of the workings to Sheffield will provide a more than adequate service.

Charles Roberts — Procor — Bombardier PRL

In the triangle created by the Horbury fork, are the works of Bombardier PRL Ltd, perhaps better known to older readers as Charles Roberts or the younger generation as Procor UK. The company dates from 1856 when Charles Roberts commenced a railway

Right:
Crofton lost its passenger station as long ago as November 1931, though the goods yard was to linger on for a further 21 years. However, the busy sidings nearby remained a principal marshalling area for coal trains in the Wakefield district right up until the opening of Healey Mills marshalling yard. By the end of 1964 most of the Crofton's traffic had been diverted to Healey Mills, but the sidings continue to fulfil a useful role as a Civil Engineering Depot. In October 1991 the depot's Class 08 shunter, No 08662, is seen at rest after the Saturday morning shift knocked off for lunch.
Author

Below:
Perhaps the most important flow of traffic on the L&YR was coal — the staple fuel for the industrial north, the heating source for most households, a basic element in the production of gas, and the very food on which steam engines themselves existed. The development of railways into the coalfields was something of a war, and the L&YR were eager combatants when it came to making incursions into the rich coalfields of South Yorkshire. After the demise of main line steam, a surviving Class 3F 0-6-0 'Jinty', in service with the NCB, propels a load of coal wagons from Calder Grove open cast site towards Flockton sidings on the Barnsley branch; the date is 3 April 1969.
Peter A. Hogarth

wagon manufacturing business at Ings Road, Wakefield. With a customer-base solidly established in the coal industry, the firm moved to larger premises off the L&YR line at Horbury Junction in 1876. In 1885 the firm built the L&YR's first spring buffer wagon and, still bearing plate No 1, this vehicle has been preserved in the National Railway Museum Collection. Expansion was seen with the establishment of a wheel-making shop in 1905 and a foundry in 1913, facilities which were well used during World War 1.

After World War 2, about 50% of the company's output went for export, and as the business continued to grow it was decided to divide the manufacturing and vehicle leasing operations. Charles Roberts Engineering Ltd remained on the site and is still operational today, having diversified into a wide range of product areas — in particular low-pressure road vehicle tank wagons. In 1970 the rail hire section was sold to the firm of Procor (UK) Ltd, a subsidiary of the Trans Union Corporation of America. They had started acquiring wagon-leasing operations, an arrangement which has already been discussed in connection with Standard Wagon of Heywood. Then, in 1977, Procor acquired the rail manufacturing side of Charles Roberts Engineering Ltd, and what had been the repair and maintenance shops for the hire fleet became a manufacturing facility for new vehicles. Ten years later Procor Engineering Ltd was formed creating two separate companies. In 1990 the manufacturing business was taken over by Bombardier Inc, and thus became Bombardier Pro-rail Ltd.

The Dearne Valley Railway

By way of conclusion we will look at one interesting little section of the L&YR empire which was promoted into the coalfield down the Dearne Valley. The L&YR branch left the WP&GR at Crofton South Junction and ran down to Ryhill, from where it ran roughly parallel with the Midland line as far as Shafton. It then joined the nominally independent Dearne Valley Railway, which commenced at Brierley Junction on the Hull & Barnsley line, curved southwest to Shafton

Left:
Darton was one of a number of intermediate stations on the Wakefield-Barnsley line. Although the stations at Crigglestone and Haigh closed on 13 September 1965, that at Darton remained open. Its facilities were, however, considerably reduced from those pictured in this early 20th century view.
B. C. Lane Collection

Below left:
During 1991 a new station was constructed at Darton. It is pictured here on 6 August 1991 with Class 144 No 144017 on the 14.42 service to Leeds. Pictured in the red and cream livery of West Yorkshire PTA, the unit was formed of three cars. *John Bateman*

Below:
Coal was the Dearne Valley Railway's *raison d'être*, but the Kirkgate-Edlington passenger service was a delightful excursion as it was a trip which included a crossing of the River Don by the spectacular 21-arch Conisbrough viaduct. This service was one which stemmed from the Hughes railmotor development and was worked in an economical fashion, with some of the stations consisting of no more than ground level platforms built from sleepers and furnished with demounted coach bodies for waiting rooms. On 29 June 1933 railmotor No 10616 is pictured at Edlington just a few months before the trailer coach was withdrawn and scrapped.
H. C. Casserley

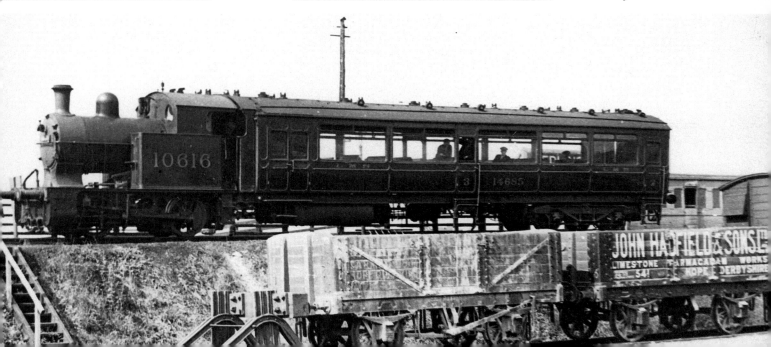

Like Castleford, Barnsley was one of the centres of the Yorkshire coal trade and an impressive network of lines developed in the region. The first line to reach the town was that promoted by the Sheffield, Rotherham, Barnsley, Wakefield, Huddersfield & Goole Railway, which opened from Horbury on 1 January 1850. This line eventually passed to the L&YR, though other companies to serve the town were the Midland and Great Central. Pictured at a barren southbound platform at Barnsley is a two-car DMU, Nos 51840 and 52067, on 22 October 1985 *en route* to Sheffield.
J. Critchley

Below right:

After the widespread withdrawals of the 1960s, passenger trains through Barnsley were largely confined to a Sheffield-Barnsley-Wakefield-Leeds DMU service. This remained the position until 1983, when the Huddersfield-Sheffield workings were diverted from Penistone — running down the GCR line which had last seen a scheduled passenger service in 1959. Working one of the Sheffield-Leeds trains, a Class 156 cascaded from the trans-Pennine routes passes through Barnsley on 13 August 1991. In the intervening six years a new station building has been added to the southbound platform.
John Bateman

and then ran via Grimethorpe, Great Houghton, Goldthorpe, Barnburgh, Denaby, Conisbrough and Edlington to the south of Doncaster. There it made connections with a number of other lines, including the GCR, GER, GNR, MR and NER, and it also provided a useful link to the South Yorkshire Joint Railway (GCR, GNR, L&YR, MR & NER joint) which ran from the Great Central line at Kirk Sandall to Dinnington. The Dearne Valley Railway was a late arrival and it did not open until 1909, while passenger services were a further three years in coming and were principally worked by Hughes railmotors from the outset. After the railmotors the service was worked by push-pull fitted 2-4-2Ts, and remarkably it lasted until June

1951. Much of the track had gone by the end of 1966, and today just isolated sections remain to serve local collieries, but given the current political attitude towards the coal mining industry one surmises that they have little future.

It would be easy to end on such a negative note, but the old L&YR system is still very much alive and kicking, and while large chunks (such as the Dearne Valley) have been decimated in the past three decades, the final years of the 20th century seem to have positively encouraging signs. This, and the fact that the ex-L&YR lines still have a considerable level of public support, just goes to prove that they were built where they were needed - long may it remain so!